P9-CED-646

THE EVERYDAY
MEDITATOR

THE EVERYDAY MEDITATOR

A PRACTICAL GUIDE

OSHO

Charles E. Tuttle Company, Inc.
Boston • Rutland, Vermont • Tokyo

A LABYRINTH BOOK

First published in the United States in 1993
by Charles E. Tuttle Company, Inc. of Rutland, Vermont & Tokyo, Japan,
with editorial offices at 77 Central Street, Boston, Massachusetts 02109.

Produced by Labyrinth Publishing (UK) Ltd
Illustrations and design by Carmen Strider

Text copyright © 1989 by Labyrinth Publishing (UK) Ltd
Original illustrations copyright © 1989 Labyrinth Publishing (UK) Ltd
All rights reserved. No part of this publication may be reproduced, stored in a
retrieval system or transmitted in any form or by any means, electronic,
mechanical, photocopying, recording, or otherwise, without prior written
permission from the publisher.

ISBN 0-8048-1976-9
Library of Congress Catalog Card Number 93-60090

First edition
Color separation by Fotolito Toscana, Italy
Typesetting by Linograf, Italy
Printed in Hong Kong

The publisher accepts no responsibility concerning
the effects of any of the techniques mentioned in this book.

The main text in this book has been set in two different type sizes,
the larger type indicates words that are taken directly from the works
of OSHO quoted mainly from the following books:
The Orange Book,
Meditation: The First and Last Freedom,
The Divine Melody,
The Search

CONTENTS

More frail and illusory
Than numbers written on water,
Our seeking from the Buddha
Felicity in the after-world.

Ikkyu

INTRODUCTION

Any form of conscious meditation is not the real thing:
it can never be.
Deliberate attempt to meditate is not meditation.
It must happen; it cannot be invited.
Meditation is not the play of the mind nor of desire and pleasure.
All attempt to meditate is the very denial of it.
Only be aware of what you are thinking and doing
and nothing else.
The seeing, the hearing, is the doing,
without reward and punishment.

J. Krishnamurti

The ink painting opposite is of Kanzan (pronounced Han-shan) – a happy lunatic monk of the Tang Dynasty who was also a renowned Zen (Ch'an) poet. Such ink drawings were very popular, with few brush strokes and light touches of ink on a white background, representing a particular technique known as the "thrifty brush" with a frugality of ink. They were seen to represent the "suchness" of all things, the painter dispensing with everything unnecessary.

This is meditation.

Meditation has been a way of life in the Eastern world for thousands of years. But because we, in the West, have developed our thinking faculties to such a fine degree, we have had little time to appreciate the other side of the coin – the side which is fundamentally different from thinking – in fact, meditation is not-thinking.

Modern dictionary definitions prefer to call meditation "contemplation," a word which still has something to do with thinking.

Even the adept of today – the meditator – in many cases will still understand meditation to be something akin to an exercise routine – something we do, sitting on the floor, legs folded into a "lotus" position, the hands on knees, forefinger and thumb pressed together, eyes shut, for one hour each day.

It is very much the modern view that these things are to be undertaken through the same process as everything else.

We jog each day from seven to eight, we "work-out" from six to seven each evening, we have a routine for each activity – we "fit it in" between all our other processes and activities – meditation, therefore, becomes one more thing to fill up a busy day.

In this way meditation will simply become

another form of stress; something we *have* to do, and will thus only add to the exhaustion and anxiety that is already there.

This is *not* meditation.

The problem that results from slotting meditation into an already busy day is that in this way it will never be possible to sample its true power. Take a typical scenario. You are a busy woman with a job that demands your attention for the greater part of the weekday. You also have a family of two children and a husband to look after at home each early morning and evening and at weekends. You go to fitness class or a gymnasium for your body. You keep your diet balanced according to some technique or other which seems to work. At weekends you are generally tired and yet you give the time you have to your family to compensate for the lack of energy you give them during the week.

You have heard that meditation is a good technique for finding a degree of peace and rest in a busy and anxious world; so you acquire a book on the subject and you set aside an hour during your already overloaded day, to try it out.

The book tells you that meditation is a matter of stopping the thoughts that continually pass through your mind – worry, plans, fantasies, possibilities, fears – all those things you have become accustomed to. In fact, before someone told you it was possible to stop thinking – to give the mind a rest – it never occurred to you that you were thinking all the time anyway. Or if it did, that this was necessarily a problem.

But now that you think of it (!), thinking suddenly does become a problem. Worry worries you more than it did before. When you don't have anything to worry about, you start to worry about that!

So, you sit down in the appointed silent room, having kicked out the kids and the cats. You adjust the cushion on the floor, you take the position indicated in the book and you close your eyes...

Silence.

Is it working? Am I in the right position? My bottom hurts already? Did I turn the oven off? I'm cold! Why can't they stop making such a row out there? Oh God, I forgot about that appointment change for tomorrow. Stop thinking, you're supposed to be meditating.

Silence.

This meditation stuff is great, I feel better already! Maybe I can skip my aerobics class for a bit and do this instead – whoops – thinking again.

Silence.

And so on – and so on forever. Actually no one can simply stop thinking just like that. The human race has been thinking for thousands of years – how can one person, in the midst of a highly "reasonable" life, suddenly expect to enter a deep state of meditation in one deliberate "sitting"? And yet this is what most of the books and instruction classes propose.

Not-thinking doesn't work. The purpose of this book is twofold:

First, to kill most or all of the preconceptions that we have about meditation and to knock over the majority of methods that are proposed as aids to meditation. You cannot "learn" meditation – you will only learn how to think you are meditating.

Secondly to create a life in which meditation exists all the time – every hour of every day – for you. For meditation exists all around us – we only have to take hold of it.

For those who have never experienced meditation before, there are a couple of small matters to be aware of from the beginning.

Finding the beginning

We reasonable creatures in the civilized world have always to begin at the beginning! Sounds strange perhaps, but when we become accustomed to meditation, beginnings and endings cease to be of importance.

Perhaps still more strange is the idea that meditation does not begin when we sit down and "start" doing it. In fact we need to find the place where it already exists.

All this may smell just slightly of mumbo-jumbo, but perhaps the reader could keep patience for a while longer and with luck all will become clear!

Imagine a circle laid out flat in the mind's eye: on the periphery of this circle is your life – the track of your life. You are moving along this track from birth to death, these two events lying side by side at some point on the circle without a gap between them. Perhaps you are a quarter of the way around, or half, or more. Imagine your place on the circle.

Imagine now that at this point of the circle where you have found yourself you are going to break out of the circle and make a new one – change the direction of the circumference. It may only be a small change, but it will alter the entire circle – its size, its circumference, its radius – every geometrical aspect of it. In effect you will become a different person – all because you jumped the circle and made a new one.

In order to make that change you must find the beginning of the meditative place inside you and to do this you must create a new habit.

So – now to add confusion to unreasonableness – we will find this new habit by doing one of the meditations in the book! For, though you may not be aware of it yet – in fact you may already be saying what kind of a crazy book is this! – by reading this small piece of text you have already broken the circle and begun a new one!

If you are a relatively calm, slow-moving person go to the meditation in the book called "Golden Light" or the one called "Sky" and do it.

If you are a physically active person, or your life is highly stressed and full of anxiety, go to the meditations called "Dynamic" or "Kundalini" or one of the other "Active" meditations and do one of them. Do the meditation once and put all your energy into it, as though your life depended on it. Choose the one that seems best suited to your general way of life.

And when it is done and you are sitting or standing or lying still at the end, look up above your head and close your eyes and see the circles – the two circles – the old one which is now a shadow and the new one which is still linked to the old but which is stronger and in a different place. Now you have found the beginning and you will never look back.

Care fullness

The second matter to be aware of is that meditation and the change of this magic circle are going to change *you*. After getting into the techniques in this book you will find things happening to you that you do not expect. In fact, the more unexpected the changes the better you are doing. If you put one hundred percent of yourself into the meditations you will notice a number of things happening.

You may become depressed, afraid, more anxious, angry with everyone about you. You may notice strong physical changes such as aches and pains, headaches, neck aches, colds, extreme tiredness. You may, on the other hand, notice

Meditation is danger for it destroys everything,
nothing whatsoever is left, not even a whisper of desire,
and in this vast, unfathomable emptiness
there is creation and love.

J. Krishnamurti

periods of great elation, surprise, calm, happiness, peace, and your body may feel light and healthy, powerful and fit. Illnesses that you are normally prone to may disappear altogether and you may find yourself so physically energetic that you need only short periods of sleep. And all this will happen at a level that you cannot control and that you do not expect. It will all be something of a surprise.

Some meditations will produce greater and more dramatic effects than others, such as the "Dynamic" and "Kundalini" meditations, but all of them will bring some effect or other and it is useful to be aware that you must expect the unexpected. Tell your closest relations or friends that you are doing this new "thing" and that they should not be surprised if you do not respond in the "normal" way.

When they react by saying that "you always were a bit crazy anyway" don't worry about it – people, even the best of friends and relations, often find changes in others alarming. If you change it may mean that they have to as well and this they may find frightening.

Most of all, though, watch over yourself and do not be afraid if things are not what you think they "ought" to be. Of course, if you suffer severe physical or anxiety problems the same applies as in any other new technique or life-style – go see your doctor and make sure that you are fit enough to follow the methods.

So now – enough advice.

If you don't use ordinary life as a method to meditation, your meditation is bound to become something of an escape.

As you go deeper into meditation time disappears. When meditation has really bloom-ed no time is found. It happens simultaneously: when the mind disappears, time disappears. Hence, down the ages, the mystics have said that time and mind are nothing but two aspects of the same coin. Mind cannot live without time and time cannot live without mind. Time is a way for the mind to exist.

Hence all the Buddhas have insisted, live in this moment: to live in this moment is meditation; to be simply here now is meditation. Those who are simply here now this very moment with me are in meditation. This is meditation – the cuckoo calling from far away and the airplane passing and the crows and the birds and all is silent and there is no movement in the mind.

You are not thinking of the past and you are not thinking of the future. Time has stopped. The world has stopped.

Stopping the world is the whole art of meditation. And to live in the moment is to live in eternity. To taste the moment with no idea, with no mind, is to taste immortality.

Meditation comes into existence only when you have looked into all motives and found them lacking, when you have gone through the whole round of motives and you have seen the falsity of it. You have seen that the motives lead nowhere, that you go on moving in circles; you remain the same. The motives go on and on leading you, driving you, almost driving you mad, creating new desires, but nothing is ever achieved. The hands remain as empty as ever. When this has been seen, when you have looked into your life and seen all your motives failing...

No motive has ever succeeded, no motive has ever brought any blessing to anybody. The motives only promise; the goods are never delivered. One motive fails and another motive comes in and promises you again ... and you are deceived again.

Being deceived again and again by motives, one day suddenly you become aware – suddenly you *see* into it, and that very seeing is the beginning of meditation. It has no seed in it, it has no motive in it. If you are meditating *for something*, then you are concentrating, not meditating. Then you are still in the world – your mind is still interested in cheap things, in trivia. Then you are worldly. Even if you are meditating to attain to God, you are worldly. Even if you are meditating to attain to nirvana, you are worldly – because meditation has no goal.

Meditation is an insight that all goals are false. Meditation is an understanding that desires don't lead anywhere.

Noticing that his father was growing old, the son of a burglar asked his father to teach him the trade, so that he could carry on the family business after his father had retired.

The father agreed, and that night they broke into a house together.

Opening a large chest the father told his son to go in and pick out the clothing.

As soon as the boy was inside, the father locked the chest and then made a lot of noise so that the whole house was aroused. Then he slipped quietly away.

Locked inside the chest the boy was angry, terrified, and puzzled as to how he was going to get out. Then an idea flashed to him – he made a noise like a cat.

The family told a maid to take a candle and examine the chest.

When the lid was unlocked the boy jumped out, blew out the candle, pushed his way past the astonished maid, and ran out. The people ran after him.

Noticing a well by the side of the road the boy threw in a large stone, then hid in the darkness. The pursuers gathered around the well trying to see the burglar drowning himself.

When the boy got home he was very angry at his father and he tried to tell him the story; but the father said: "Don't bother to tell me the details, you are here – you have learned the art."

MORNING

I laugh when I hear that the fish in the water is thirsty:
Why so impatient, my heart?
He who watches over the birds, beasts and insects,
he who cared for you whilst you were yet in your mother's womb,
shall he not care for you now that you have come forth?
O my heart, how could you turn from the smile of
your Lord and wander so far from Him?
You have left your Beloved and are thinking of others:
and this is why all your work is in vain.

Kabir

The morning is a particularly sensitive time. Sleep and the warmth and intimacy of the bed create a great sensitivity in the body and the moment we wake up it is a great surprise to come back to the day again.

For some of us it might even be a great shock! But after years of getting up in the same, habitual fashion, we become accustomed to ignoring the feelings that arise first thing after waking. Perhaps it is depression, perhaps it is great pleasure and happiness. But the work has to be done – the day must be faced so the sensitivity disappears and we plunge headlong into our normal activities and forget what we felt on waking.

OK, so there isn't time. There's never time – time is the biggest con trick in the civilized world.

Wake up ten minutes earlier – the day will be completely different if you follow these morning meditations.

Laughing out

The first thing to be done is laughter,
because that sets the trend for the whole day.
If you wake up laughing,
you will soon begin to feel how absurd life is.
Nothing is serious: even your disappointments are laughable,
even your pain is laughable, even you are laughable.

OSHO

Usually, as soon as we wake up, all the daily worries and activities – preparing breakfast, getting ready for work, rushing to catch the bus and so on – crowd our minds and bring with them seriousness and tension. For most of us, this is a normal way of life and we might not even imagine that there is anything to do about it. But there is.

Change this habit. Allow yourself just ten or fifteen minutes every morning to try this meditation. It will fill your being with a bubbling, joyous energy that will spread all over you and your daily activities.

Every morning upon waking, before opening your eyes, stretch like a cat. Stretch every fiber of your body. After three or four minutes, with eyes still closed, begin to laugh. For five minutes just laugh. At first you will be doing it, but soon the sound of your attempt will cause genuine laughter. Lose yourself in laughter. It may take several days before it really happens, for we are so unaccustomed to the phenomenon. But before long it will be spontaneous and will change the whole nature of your day.

Your own song

Let things alone and labor not to change them.
For they seem what they seem only because you seem what you seem.
They neither see nor speak except you lend them sight and speech.

Mikhail Naimy, *The Book of Mirdad*

The laughing meditation has filled you with such joy and lightness that you might spontaneously start singing while taking your shower or cooking pancakes for your breakfast.

Whenever a song arises in you, at any time of the day or night, lose your self-consciousness, don't worry about what the neighbors might say, probably they will appreciate your song anyway, so remember this.

Singing is divine, one of the most divine activities. You can drown yourself in singing, so much so that the singer disappears, only the song remains. And that is the moment of metamorphosis, transfiguration, when the singer is no more and there is only the song.

When your totality has become a song or a dance, that is prayer.

What song you are singing is irrelevant; it may not be a religious song, but if you can sing it totally it is sacred. The content of the song does not matter; what matters is the quality that you bring to singing, the totality, the intensity, the fire.

Don't repeat anybody else's song, because that is not your heart, and that is not the way you can pour your heart at the divine feet. Let your own song arise. Forget about meter and grammar. God is not too much of a grammarian, and He is not worried about what words you use. He is more concerned about your heart.

Funny faces

Freedom is emptying the mind of experience.
When the brain ceases to nourish itself through experience,
then its activity is not self-centered.
It then has its nourishment that makes the mind religious.

J. Krishnamurti

This is a very ancient technique of meditation used in Tibet for centuries. It can be done in your room or in your bathroom, in front of a big mirror, after or before you take your shower.

It is a very simple, fun meditation yet you will be surprised at the taste of freedom it will give you. You will soon come to experience that you are not your body, that your body does not confine you, but it is just a beautiful tool to play with. This insight will bring detachment and coolness into your life.

Keep a big mirror. Stand naked, make faces, do funny things – and watch. Just doing it and watching for 15-20 minutes, you will be surprised. You will start feeling you are separate from this. If you are not separate then how can you do all these things? Then the body is just in your hand, is just something in your hand. You can play with it this way and that. Find out new ways to make funny faces, funny postures. Do whatever you can do and it will give you a great release and you will start looking at yourself, not as the body, not as the face, but as the consciousness. It will be helpful.

Sunrising

The flower is the form, the scent, the color
and the beauty that is the whole of it.
Tear it to pieces actually or verbally, then there is no flower,
only a remembrance of what it was, which is never the flower.
Meditation is the whole flower in its beauty,
withering and living.

J. Krishnamurti

Just fifteen minutes before the sun rises, when the sky is becoming a little lighter, just wait and watch as one waits for a beloved: so tense, so deeply awaiting, so hopeful and excited – and yet silent. No need to stare, you can blink your eyes. Have a feeling that simultaneously inside something is also rising.

When the sun comes on the horizon, start feeling that it is just near the navel. It comes up over there, and here, inside the navel, it comes up, comes up slowly. The sun is rising there, and here an inner point of light is rising. Just ten minutes will do, then close your eyes. When you first see the sun with open eyes, it creates a negative so when you close your eyes, you can see the sun dazzling inside.

And this is going to change you tremendously.

Gazing

Yours is a world divided 'gainst itself,
because the "I" in you is so divided.
Yours is a world of barriers and fences,
because the "I" in you is one of barriers and fences.
Some things it would fence out as alien to itself.
Some things it would fence in as kindred to itself.
Yet that outside the fence is ever breaking in;
and that within the fence is ever breaking out.

Mikhail Naimy, *The Book of Mirdad*

The technique of gazing is not concerned really with the object, it is concerned with the gazing itself. Because when you stare without blinking your eyes, you become focussed, and the nature of the mind is to be constantly moving. If you are really gazing, not moving at all, the mind is bound to be in difficulty.

The nature of the mind is to move from one object to another, to move constantly. If you are gazing at darkness or at light or at something else, if you are really gazing, the movement of the mind stops. Because if the mind goes on moving, your gaze will not be there; you will go on missing the object.

There are many different methods of using the art of gazing as a meditation. You can gaze at a candle; at a crystal or a crystal ball; at a partner, sitting across from each other, looking into each other's left eye; at a photo of a guru; or any other object. One of the best and perhaps most neglected methods is gazing at yourself.

Take a mirror and place it against a wall where you can sit comfortably on a cushion on the floor. Shut the door and turn out the lights but leave a single candle beside the mirror in such a way as to be able to see your face without any glare from the candle. Now look at your face and notice everything about it as though this were someone else. Suspend the usual judgments about how pretty or ugly or tired you are. Simply gaze at yourself. You will be surprised how much pleasure there is in this.

Gaze into your own eyes without blinking. Let your eyes run or burn a little, relax into that feeling until you do not blink at all. Keep this up for forty minutes each day for two weeks. Do not give up and you will find that your face changes its

shape, its expressions. It becomes as though it is not your face at all. But these different faces are all your own faces and you will be surprised how many there are of them.

After two weeks, if you keep staring you will find that you do not need to blink at all and eventually something truly magical will come about. Your face will disappear in the mirror. You will not be there at all. At this very moment close your eyes and you will be in touch with your unconscious in its purest form – without deception – the naked you.

In the same way you can gaze at any other thing and you will be surprised what happens to you.

Margaret Anderson relates in her book, *The Unknowable Gurdjieff*, that Gurdjieff used to play his small accordion-piano in the evenings. One evening, however, he played "a different kind of music, although whether the difference lay in its sorrowful harmonies or in the way he played, I do not know. I only know that no music had ever been so sad. Before it ended I put my head on the table and wept.

"'What has happened to me?' I said. 'When I came into this room I was was happy. And then that music – and now I am happy again.'

"'I play objective music to cry,' Gurdjieff said. 'There are many kinds of such music – some to make laugh, or to love or to hate...'"

This could be defined as an "objective art" meditation. The only thing required from you is to have a Buddha statue either in your room or in your work place and look at it whenever you feel the need of centering yourself into a peaceful and harmonious space.

The Buddha statue was not created just as an image; it was created as an object for meditation. It does not represent the real Buddha – he was not like that. It is a metaphor. Rather than representing the Buddha's physical shape it represents his inner grace. It was not that he was just of the same physical shape, the same face, the same nose and eyes; that is not at all the point. It is not realistic – it is surrealistic. It says something of the real that is beyond the so-called reality.

Just looking at it one can fall into meditation. There are temples that have ten thousand Buddha statues just to create an atmosphere of meditativeness ... the Buddha being, that silence, that grace, those closed eyes, that still posture, that balance, that symmetry. Those Buddha statues are music in marble, sermons in stones.

Running through

Meditation is this attention in which there is an awareness,
without choice of the movement of all things, the cawing of the crows,
the trembling of the leaves, the noisy stream, a boy calling,
the feelings, the motives, the thoughts chasing each other and going
deeper, the awareness of total consciousness.

J. Krishnamurti

You might not think of running as a meditation, but runners sometimes have felt a tremendous experience of meditation. And they were surprised because they were not looking for it. Who thinks that a runner is going to experience God? But it has happened...

It can happen when running. If you have ever been a runner, if you have enjoyed running in the morning when the air is fresh and young and the whole world is coming back from sleep, awakening ... everything singing all around, you are feeling so alive, a moment comes when the runner disappears and there is only running. The body, mind and soul start functioning together, suddenly an inner orgasm is released!

Runners have sometimes come accidentally on a mystical experience, although they will miss it – they will think it was just because of running that they enjoyed the moment, that it was a beautiful day, the body was healthy and the world was beautiful, and it was just a certain mood ... a runner can come close to meditation more easily than anybody else.

Jogging can be of immense help, swimming can be of immense help. All these things have to be transformed into meditation.

...Start running in the morning on the road. Start with half a mile and then one mile and come eventually to at least three miles. While running use the whole body. Don't run as if you are in a straitjacket. Run like a small child, using the whole body, hands and feet, and run. Breathe deeply and from the belly. Then sit under a tree, rest, perspire and let the cold breeze come. Feel peaceful. This will help you very deeply.

Sometimes just stand on the earth without shoes and feel the coolness, the softness, the warmth. Whatever the earth is ready to give at that moment, just feel it and let it flow through you. And allow your energy to flow into the earth. Be connected with the earth.

If you are connected with the earth, you are connected with life. If you are connected with the earth, you are connected with your body. If you are connected with the earth, you will become very sensitive and centered – and that's what is needed.

Never become an expert in running, remain an amateur so that alertness may be kept. If you feel sometimes that running has become automatic, drop it, try swimming. If that becomes automatic, then dancing. The point to remember is that movement is just a situation to create awareness. While it creates awareness it is good, if it stops creating awareness, then it is no more of any use. Change to another movement where you will have to be alert again.

Never allow any activity to become automatic.

Stop still

Stopping the world is the whole art of meditation.
And to live in the moment is to live in eternity.
To taste the moment with no idea, with no mind,
is to taste immortality.

OSHO

How often have we become upset while, rushing to work, we walk on crowded streets and we are bumped by others as hurried as ourselves? The irritation caused by this makes us wish we were not there, but somewhere else, with no people around us. Yet, even such an ordinary and upsetting situation can become a meditation, if only we do not escape from it, but use it with awareness.

Next time you are walking in the rush hour and you feel yourself getting upset, try this method.

Walking on the street – suddenly you remember. Stop yourself completely, no movement. Just be present for half a minute. Whatsoever the situation, stop completely and just be present to whatsoever is happening. Then start moving again. Six times a day.

If you just become present suddenly, the whole energy changes. The continuity that was going on in the mind stops. And it is so sudden that the mind cannot create a new thought so immediately. It takes time; the mind is stupid.

Anywhere, the moment you remember, just give a jerk to your whole being and stop. Not only will you become aware. Soon you will feel that others have become aware of your energy – that something has happened; something from the unknown is entering you.

Work-wise

*To be a Tathagata (an enlightened one) is to dance the day
instead of working it.
The "curse of work" that came from the Fall
was the supposition that one "must" live.*

Alan Watts

A greater part of most of our lives is spent working, yet how many of us really enjoy working? It seems we take work as a duty and wait for the weekends or the holidays to finally relax and enjoy ourselves. If only we could bring a contented relaxation into our work we might discover that work is actually not work, but is both pleasure and meditation!

This very simple method will help you bring a new quality – the quality of enjoyment and relaxation – into your work. Follow it as often as you can and soon you will see that there is no difference between typing a letter and playing with your children at home!

Whenever you feel that you are not in a good mood and you don't feel good in the work, before starting work, just for five minutes, exhale deeply. Feel with the exhalation that you are throwing your dark mood out ... within five minutes you will be suddenly back to normal and the low will have disappeared, the dark is no more there.

...It is simply a shift of emphasis; nothing much to be done. Things that you have been doing carelessly, start doing carefully. Things that you have been doing for some results ... just bringing love to it will reap many more things which otherwise you would miss.

Vice versa

Let man be free from pleasure and let man be free from pain;
for not to have pleasure is sorrow and to have pain is also sorrow.
From pleasure arises sorrow and from pleasure arises fear.
If a man is free from pleasure, he is free from fear and sorrow.

Buddha, *The Dhammapada*

Pleasure and pain, anger and compassion seem to us to be things very distinct from each other. We seek pleasure, shy away from pain; we wish to be compassionate and not angry.

This is one of the most basic misunderstandings of our life. Pleasure and pain are just two aspects of the same coin. At one time the tossed coin shows pain, another time it might just as easily show pleasure; if we toss compassion, anger is just on the other side.

Whenever this division comes up in you, try this meditation. You will discover that you can, at will, swing from one to the other. This discovery will be soon followed by another one – that actually *you* are neither.

This is a beautiful method. It will be very useful. For example: if you are feeling very discontented, what to do? Ponder on the opposite. If you are feeling discontented, contemplate about contentment. What is contentment? Bring a balance. If your mind is angry, bring compassion in, think about compassion; and immediately the energy changes, because they are the same. The opposite is the same energy... Anger is there, contemplate on compassion.

Do one thing: keep a statue of Buddha, because that statue is the gesture of compassion. Whenever you feel angry ... look at Buddha ... and feel compassion. Suddenly you will see a transformation happening within you. The anger is changing: excitement gone, compassion arising. And it is not different energy. It is the same energy – the same energy as anger – changing its quality, going higher. Try it!

Real meeting

There never was, there never will be,
nor is there now,
a man whom men always blame,
or a man whom they always praise.

Buddha, *The Dhammapada*

So engrossed are we with our own thoughts, worries and anxieties that very rarely do we meet someone, for business or any other reason, with clean, unjudging eyes and with an open heart.

Thus this so-called "meeting" is just a reflection of our tense minds and we are then unable to really see and come into contact with the other person.

This very simple method can help you immensely in all your relationships.

When somebody comes to see you or meets you, just settle within yourself, become silent. When the man enters, deep down feel peace for him. Feel: "Peace be to this man." Don't just say it, feel it. Suddenly you will see a change in the man as if something unknown had entered into his being. He will be totally different.

Golden light

If you were in the presence of God, what would you say?
I don't know!
Good, very good.

Anonymous

This is a simple method of transforming your energy and leading it upwards. The process is to be done at least twice a week.

The best time is early in the morning, just before you get up from your bed. The moment you feel you are alert, awake, do it for twenty minutes. Do it then and there, immediately, because when you are coming out of sleep you are very fresh and the impact will go very deep. When you are just coming out of sleep, you are less in the mind than ever, hence some gaps are there through which the method will penetrate into your innermost core. And early in the morning, when you are awakening and when the whole earth is awakening, there is a great tide of awakening energy all over... – use that tide, don't miss that opportunity!

...You simply lie down as you are lying down on your bed, on your back. Keep your eyes closed. When you breathe in, just visualize a great light entering through your head into your body, as if a sun has risen just close to your head. You are hollow and the golden light is pouring into your head and going in, going in, deep, deep and going out through your toes.

When you breathe in, do it with this visualization – the golden light will help, it will cleanse your whole body and will make it absolutely full of creativity. This is male energy.

And when you breathe out, visualize another thing: darkness entering through your toes, a great, dark river entering through your toes, coming up and going out from your head. Do slow, deep breathing so you can visualize. This is feminine energy.

It will soothe you, it will make you receptive, it will calm you, it will give you rest. Go very slowly and just out of sleep, you can have very deep and slow breaths because the body is rested, relaxed.

If you do this simple method for three months, you will be surprised ... transformation has started happening.

 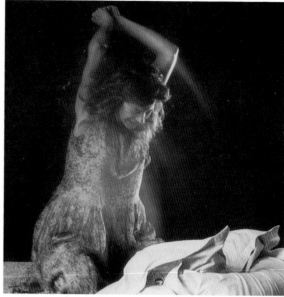

Pillow-bashing

*Meditation is the freeing of energy in abundance;
and control, discipline and suppression spoil the purity
of that energy.*

J. Krishnamurti

The whole emphasis of this method is in expressing your anger, your frustration, your negativity before it becomes a pattern in your life. Usually we bottle up all these feelings until the moment they explode, more often than not towards somebody who has actually nothing to do with it.

Next time, before exploding, wait a little. Go into your room, take a pillow and try this experiment – it is actually like taking a shower! You wash away all the dust that has gathered upon your consciousness.

When you feel angry, there is no need to be angry against someone, just be angry. Let it be a meditation. Close the room, sit by yourself,

and let the anger come up as much as it can. If you feel like beating, beat a pillow.

Do whatsoever you want to do; the pillow will never object. If you want to kill the pillow, have a knife and kill it! It helps, it helps tremendously. One can never imagine how helpful a pillow can be. Just beat it, bite it, throw it. If you are against somebody in particular, write their name on the pillow or stick a picture on it.

You will feel ridiculous, foolish, but anger is ridiculous; you cannot do anything about it. So let it be and enjoy it like an energy phenomenon. It *is* an energy phenomenon. If you are not hurting anybody, there is nothing wrong in it. When you try this you will see that the idea of hurting somebody by and by disappears.

Make it a daily practice – just twenty minutes every morning. Then watch the whole day. You will be calm because the energy that becomes anger has been thrown out; the energy that becomes a poison is thrown out of the system. Do this for at least two weeks, and after one week you will be surprised to find that whatsoever the situation, anger is not coming up. Just give it a try.

Pillow-bashing is completely familiar to children – especially those who have been to boarding school. Children do not hesitate to express their feelings of anger or frustration and bashing a pillow is a sure way of having fun with feelings. Adults have the idea that such things are not grown-up – and they're right – but who wants to be grown-up all the time? One of the biggest reasons for social unrest and problems is the fact that people prefer to keep their angry feelings quiet. If governments around the world were to make pillow-bashing compulsory, crime would drop rapidly!

AFTERNOON

Do not go to the garden of flowers! O Friend! Go not there,
In your body is the garden of flowers.
Take your seat on the thousand petals of the lotus,
and there gaze on the Infinite Beauty.

Kabir

We happily separate our day into sections – morning, afternoon, evening, lunch time, dinner time. We have periods of high and low energy, however, which fortunately refuse to fit into these man-made compartments and resolutely continue to puzzle us by occurring at "odd-times" – i.e. times that we cannot fit into our self-imposed patterns.

Meditation loves "odd-times" as it encompasses the natural flow of the body. It can therefore happily be there at the lowest and the highest of moments.

Open-handed

What is this day with two suns in the sky?
Day unlike other days,
with a great voice giving it to the planet,
Here it is, enamored beings, your day!

Rumi

"At other times, the memory has much a deeper dimension – a sensation of being immeasurably ancient and knowing, as somehow prior to time and space. But there is nothing at all specific about it, for though the sensation is vivid, it is tantalizingly ephemeral. These are, then, intimations of something to be remembered which is, as it were, a vast dimension of one's being which has been kept hidden – perhaps from the moment of birth. For consciousness, or conscious attention, is the trick of noticing the figure and ignoring the background, and in the same way I seem to notice the ego and forget my background, the larger Self which underlies the ego." Alan Watts.

Another of these unusual actions it never occurs to us to perform – very very simple but enormously rewarding – especially if you are a hard-working business person.

If you place your hands into the posture of a cup, like a receptacle, it is very meaningful. It makes you receptive, it helps you to be receptive. It is one of the old, ancient postures – all Buddhas have tried it. Whenever you are open, or you want to be open, this posture will help.

Sit silently and wait. Be a receptacle, a receiving end. Just as you wait on the phone: you have rung, you wait on the phone. Exactly in that mood simply wait, and within two, three minutes you will see a totally different energy surrounding you, filling your inside, falling into you like rain falls on the earth and goes on penetrating deeper and the earth soaks it...

There is a kind of softness and inner warmth and relief that results from such an unlikely and simple act. Try doing it often during your hectic day and you'll be surprised how much energy you will receive – it's all out there waiting for you after all.

Inner smile

If thine eye be single, thy whole body shall be full of light.

Proverb

This is a technique that can be experimented with whenever you have a few minutes free. Sitting in a park after your lunch, resting for a few minutes in your garden or anywhere else, try it and a feeling of soft, peaceful contentment will spread all over you and overflow into your activities.

Whenever you are sitting and you have nothing to do, just relax your lower jaw and open the mouth just slightly. Start breathing from the mouth but not deeply. Just let the body breathe so it will be shallow and will be more and more shallow. And when you feel that the breathing has become very shallow and the mouth is open and your jaw is relaxed, your whole body will feel very relaxed.

In that moment, start feeling a smile – not on the face but all over your inner being ... It is not a smile that comes on the lips – it is an existential smile that spreads just inside.

Try and you will know what it is ... because it cannot be explained. No need to smile with the lips on the face but just as if you are smiling from the belly; the belly is smiling. And it is a smile, not a laughter, so it is very very soft, delicate, fragile – like a small rose flower opening in the belly and the fragrance spreading all over the body.

Once you have known what this smile is you can remain happy for twenty-four hours. And whenever you feel that you are missing that happiness, just close your eyes and catch hold of that smile again and it will be there ... it is always there.

Smoking meditation

It is easy to do what is wrong, to do what is bad for oneself;
but very difficult to do what is right,
to do what is good for oneself.

Buddha, *The Dhammapada*

One of the "obligations" that Gurdjieff gave to his disciples was, "preserve your life" which meant "be just to the body, satisfy its needs; treat it as a good master treats a good servant." It seems an easy task, yet if we do pay attention to how we treat our bodies we will discover that we actually mistreat them most of the time.

And why do we mistreat them so? Mainly it is because we have become fixed into mechanical habits. Let's take smoking as an example. Are we aware when we light and smoke a cigarette? Would we be able to say how many puffs we have taken or how many cigarettes we have smoked during the day?

This is the technique that gives you the key for quitting smoking: an undivided, unwavering attention.

Do one thing: when you are taking the packet of cigarettes out of your pocket, move slowly. Enjoy it, there is no hurry. Be conscious, alert, aware; take it out slowly, with full awareness. Then take the cigarette out of the packet with full awareness, slowly – not in the old hurried way, unconscious way, mechanical way. Then start tapping the cigarette on your packet – but very alertly. Listen to the sound, just as Zen people do when the tea starts boiling.

Then put it in your mouth, with full awareness, light it with full awareness. Enjoy every act, every small act, and divide it into as many small acts as possible, so you can become more and more aware.

Then have the first puff: God in the form of smoke ... Fill your lungs deeply then release the smoke, relax, another puff – and go very slowly.

If you can do it you will be surprised; soon you will see the whole stupidity of it. Not because others have said that it is stupid, not because others have said that is is bad. *You* will see it.

This is the secret, *the* secret: de-automatize.

Good waiting

All meditation is waiting, all prayer is infinite patience...
If you can persuade the mind to wait you will be in prayer,
because waiting means no thinking.

OSHO

In our civilized world we have many opportunities for waiting. We wait for buses and trains, for love, for work, for happiness and for success. With such a premium on time it is often the case that we hate to wait, for we think that somehow life will suddenly end before we get there! It is hard for us to stop and consider just how little rush there really is. One of Georges Gurdjieff's favorite maxims was "never hurry" – regardless of the motivation – never hurry – what an idea for modern society!

But the biggest sadness about all this rushing and pushing is that we don't enjoy waiting – here is a way you can.

Sometimes what happens is that meditation is close by but you are engaged in other things. That still small voice is within you but you are full of noise, engagements, occupations, responsibilities. And meditation comes like a whisper, it doesn't come like a slogan shouting, it comes very silently. It makes no noise. Not even the footsteps are heard. So if you are engaged, it waits and goes.

So ... just sit silently and wait for it. Don't do anything, just sit silently with closed eyes in great waiting, with a waiting heart, with an open heart. Just waiting...

High-light

Self-knowledge, or self-realization is to realize for yourself and by your-self that there is no self to realize – that is going to be a shattering blow.

U.G. Krishnamurti

Meditation on light is one of the most ancient meditations. In all the ages, in all the countries, in all the religions, it has been emphasized for a particular reason, because the moment you meditate on light, something inside you that has remained a bud starts opening its petals. The very meditation on light creates a space for its opening.

So let that be your meditation. Whenever you have time close your eyes; visualize light. Whenever you see light be in tune with it. Just don't go on ignoring it. Be worshipful towards it. It may be a sunrise, it may be just a candle in the room, but be prayerful towards it and you will gain much. Great is the benediction if one is feeling in tune with light.

Looking through the fog

*Meditation is opening the eyes,
meditation is looking.*

OSHO

Meditation is nothing but the art of opening your eyes, the art of cleansing your eyes, the art of dropping the dust that is gathered on the mirror of your consciousness...

The existential moment is right now. Just have a look, and that is meditation – that look is meditation...

Try in small things not to bring the mind in. You look at a flower – you simply look. Don't say "beautiful," "ugly". Don't say anything. Don't bring in words, don't verbalize. Simply look. The mind will feel uncomfortable, uneasy. The mind would like to say something. You simply say to the mind "Be silent, let me see, I will just look."

In the beginning it will be difficult, but start with things in which you are not too involved ... look at things which are neutral – a rock, a flower, a tree, the sun rising, a bird in flight, a cloud moving in the sky. Just look at things with which you are not much involved, from which you can remain detached, towards which you can remain indifferent. Start from neutral things and only then move towards emotionally loaded situations.

Listening for more

The mind of man is without sound,
Without odor;
He who answers when called
Is nothing but a thief.

Ikkyu

You have been shopping and you are tired. You sit to rest in a coffee shop, but the noise surrounding you prevents you from relaxing and you wish you were in a quiet, silent place.

Try this method. The market-place might be just the right place to be in a meditative state.

In fact, Gurdjieff used to spend afternoons sitting outside a cafe, in Paris, talking to his disciples, drinking coffee and watching people go by.

This simple method can be a finger pointing to the moon.

Remain passive – not doing anything, just listening. And listening is not a doing... Listening is a deep participation between the body and the soul and that is why it has been used as one of the most potentially powerful methods of meditation, because it bridges the two infinities: the material and the spiritual...

Whenever you are sitting, just listen to whatsoever is going on. It is the market place and there is much noise and traffic ... listen to it with no rejection in the mind that it is noisy. Listen as if you are listening to music, with sympathy. And suddenly you will see that the quality of the noise has changed. It is no more distracting, no more disturbing. On the contrary, it becomes very soothing. If listened to rightly, even the market place becomes a melody.

So what you are listening to is not the point. The point is you are listening, not just hearing.

Even if you are listening to something that you have never thought of as worth listening to, listen to it very cheerfully as if you were listening to a Beethoven sonata. And suddenly you will see that you have transformed the quality of it. It becomes beautiful. And in that listening, your ego will disappear.

The art of tea

Love your body. Be kind to it, nourish it, tender it.
It is the pure instrument of expression that allows you
to experience life on this plane.

Ramtha

Zen has transformed the most ordinary activity into meditation by bringing reverence and harmony into the smallest act.

Even if you do not have a Zen tea room, even if you are sipping your tea in your kitchen or in your living room with friends, you'll be able to experience that reverence that makes everything holy if you bring a joyous totality to it.

Ordinary tea can become extraordinarily beautiful – a tremendous experience if you enjoy it. Enjoy it with deep reverence. Make it a ceremony: making tea ... listening to the kettle and the sound, then pouring the tea ... smelling the fragrance of it; then tasting the tea and feeling happy.

Dead people cannot drink tea; only very alive people can. This moment you are alive! This moment you are drinking tea. Feel thankful!

Buddhists invented tea to help them with their meditation and it all began when Bodhidharma was once spending long hours meditating in the mountain of Ta (also known as Cha) and kept falling asleep. The sacred story is that he became so frustrated with his falling eyelids that he ripped

them off and threw them away! Thereafter they grew into flowers which when brewed with hot water made a drink that helped him and his disciples to stay awake. Tea is therefore a sacred substance for Buddhists – as well as for the English who are often still heard to say – "let's have a cuppa Cha!"

The invisible person

If there is a moment when there is
nobody who is experiencing anything,
that is the moment... you have blissful states,
ecstatic states, a sudden melting away of everything...

U.G. Krishnamurti

This is one of the most ancient meditations still used in some monasteries of Tibet. They teach that sometimes you can simply disappear; sitting in the garden, you just start feeling that you are disappearing.

Just see how the world looks when you have gone from the world, when you are no longer here, when you have become absolutely transparent. Just try for a single second not to be.

In your own home be as if you are not. It is really a beautiful meditation. You can try it many times in 24 hours – just half a second will do. For half a second simply stop; you are not and the world continues. When you become more and more alert to the fact that without you the world continues perfectly well then you will be able to learn about another part of your being which has been neglected for long, for lives. And that is the receptive mode. You simply allow, become a door.

Just sit under a tree. The breeze is blowing and the leaves of the trees are rustling. The wind touches you, it moves around you, it passes. But don't allow it just to pass you; allow it to move within you and pass through you. Just close your eyes, and as it is passing through the tree and there is a rustling of leaves, feel that you are also like a tree, open, and the wind is blowing through you – not by your side, but right through you.

The energy pillar

*This is the whole art of meditation:
how to be deep in action,
how to renounce thinking,
and how to convert the thinking
energy into awareness.*

OSHO

Would you ever imagine that waiting for the bus, or the train, or standing in a queue could be the occasion for regenerating your depleted energy?

Usually in such a situation the mind starts chattering, complaining, projecting on all the things needed to be done thus wasting the little energy we still have after a day's work.

Break this habit! Next time you are in a queue, stand quietly, do not pay any attention to the noise around you, to your mind or the chattering of the other people ... try this experiment.

A certain silence immediately comes to you if you stand quietly ... stand silently, not doing anything. Suddenly the energy also stands inside you ... standing, the energy flows like a pillar and is distributed equally all over the body. Standing is beautiful.

...Just by standing and not doing anything, not moving, you will find that something settles within you, becomes silent, the centering happens and you will feel yourself like a pillar of energy. The body disappears.

Head-quarters

*Without meditation the heart becomes a desert,
a wasteland.*

J. Krishnamurti

This is a very powerful tool to get in touch with your body's alarm system. Usually when we have a headache our automatic reaction is to go to the medicine cabinet, take some pills and forget all about it. But your headache is most probably a bell rung by your body to tell you something is not right.

Next time wait a little bit, try this experiment and see what happens.

Sit silently and watch it, look into it – not as if you are looking at an enemy, no. If you are looking at it as your enemy, you will not be able to look rightly ... Look at it as your friend. It is your friend ... it is saying, "Something is wrong – look into it."

Just sit silently and look into the headache with no idea of stopping it, with no desire that it should disappear, no conflict, no fight, no antagonism. Just look into it, into what it is.

Watch, so if there is some inner message, the headache can give it to you. It has a coded message. And if you look silently you will be surprised. If you look silently three things will happen.

First: the more you look into it, the more severe it will become. And then you will be a little puzzled, "How is it going to help if it is becoming more severe?" It is becoming more severe because you have been avoiding it. It was there but you were avoiding it; you were already repressing – even without the aspirin you were repressing it. When you look into it, repression disappears. The headache will come to its natural severity...

First thing: it will become severe. If it is becoming severe, you can be satisfied that you are looking rightly. If it does not become severe then you are not looking yet; you are still avoiding...

The second thing will be that it will become more pin-pointed; it will not be spread over a bigger space. First you were thinking, "It is my whole head aching." Now you will see it is not the whole head, it is just a small spot. That is also an indication that you are gazing more deeply into it. The spread feeling of the ache is a trick – that is a way to avoid it...

Look into it and the second step will be that it comes to be smaller and smaller and smaller. And a moment comes when it is just the very point of a needle – *very* sharp, immensely sharp, very painful. You have never seen such pain in the head. But very much confined to a small spot. Go on looking into it.

And then the third and the most important thing happens. If you go on looking at this point when it is very severe and confined and concentrated at one point, you will see many times that it disappears. When your gaze is perfect it will disappear. And when it disappears you will have the glimpse of where it is coming from – what the cause is...

And there can be a thousand and one causes. The same alarm is given because the alarm system is simple. There are not many alarm systems in your body. For different causes the same alarm is given. You may have been angry lately and you have not expressed it. Suddenly, like a revelation, it will be standing there. You will see all your anger that you have been carrying, carrying ... that anger wants to be released. It needs a catharsis. Cathart! and immediately you will see the headache has disappeared. And there was no need for the aspirin, no need for any treatment.

High-wire tension

"All is unreal". When one sees this, he is above sorrow.
This is the clear path.

Buddha, *The Dhammapada*

Once we have reacted to a certain situation or situations with anger or frustration, it becomes very easy to fall into a pattern and react to those similar situations with the same feelings again and again.

And the more angry and frustrated we are, the more often those situations will arise thus creating a vicious circle from which one can step out only with a conscious effort.

This technique will greatly help you in breaking your patterns. It is a very simple method – it takes only fifteen minutes yet you will be amazed at how different you will feel after a while. It is best done in your room so that you won't be distracted by anything and will be able to go totally into it.

Every day for fifteen minutes, any time you feel good, choose a time and close the room and become angry – but don't release it. Go on forcing it ... go almost crazy with anger, but don't release it, no expression, not even a pillow to hit. Repress it in every way...

If you feel tension arising in the stomach, as if something is going to explode, pull the stomach in, make it as tense as you can. If you feel the shoulders are becoming tense, make them more tense. Let the whole body be as tense as possible almost as if on a volcano, boiling within and with no release. That is the point to remember: no release, no expression. Don't scream, otherwise the stomach will be released. Don't hit anything, otherwise the shoulders will be released and relaxed.

For fifteen minutes get heated up as if one is at one hundred degrees. For fifteen minutes work to a climax. Put an alarm on and when the alarm goes, try the hardest you can. And as the alarm stops, sit silently, close your eyes and just watch what is happening. Relax the body.

This heating of the system will force your patterns to melt.

EVENING

When I am with you, we stay up all night.
When you are not here, I can't go to sleep.
Praise God for these two insomnias!
And the difference between them.

Rumi

Most people who work for a daily living soon get the idea that our "time-off" is so precious that we spend most of our working hours waiting for it, hungrily! Evenings and weekends become like gold nuggets to be caressed and cherished. This too can lead to problems for that "spare-time" can result in disappointments as things don't quite turn out to be as good as we had hoped. A lot of the time the problem is that we carry our tension and our anxieties from the office or the factory back home with us and then get surprised that no one likes it! Evening *is* a precious time – it is a time to let go of everything that has happened in the day that is not useful for the night.

There is the famous story of the Zen monks who were traveling through the land close to their home and came across a river. At the edge of the river was a young and beautiful woman who wanted to cross but could not swim. One of the two monks took her on his shoulders and carried her across the water, whereupon she stood down and left the monks. The other monk was furious saying to his friend that Zen monks were never to touch a woman and this monk had committed a terrible breach of his faith. Finally the two monks reached the nearby town and the complaining monk stopped and turned to his friend and said: "I will have to talk to the Master about your behavior – I will have to report it – it is prohibited." And the monk who had carried the girl answered: "What are you talking about? What is prohibited?". "Have you forgotten – you carried that young beautiful woman on your shoulders across the river." The first monk laughed and said: "Yes, I carried her, but I left her at the river miles back. You are still carrying her now."

Death: the end

*Only a person not living asks,
"What will happen after my death?"
You are not living. First live your life.*

U.G. Krishnamurti

In the night before you go to sleep, do this fifteen-minute meditation. It is a death meditation. Lie down and relax your body. Just feel like dying and that you cannot move your body because you are dead. Just create the feeling that you are disappearing from the body. Do it for ten, fifteen minutes, and you will start feeling it within a week. Meditating that way, fall asleep. Don't break it. Let the meditation turn into sleep, and if sleep overcomes you, go into it.

Life: the beginning

In the morning, the moment you feel you are awake – don't open your eyes – do the life meditation. Feel that you are becoming more wholly alive, that life is coming back and the whole body is full of vitality and energy. Start moving, swaying in the bed with eyes closed. Just feel that life is flowing in you. Feel that the body has a great flowing energy – just the opposite of the death meditation.

So do the death meditation in the night before falling asleep and the life meditation just before getting up. With the life meditation you can take deep breaths. Just feel full of energy ... life entering with breathing. Feel full and very happy, alive. Then after fifteen minutes, get up.

Paper thoughts

Only a man himself
can be the master of himself:
who else from outside
could be his master?
When the Master
and servant are one,
then there is true help
and self-possession.

Buddha, *The Dhammapada*

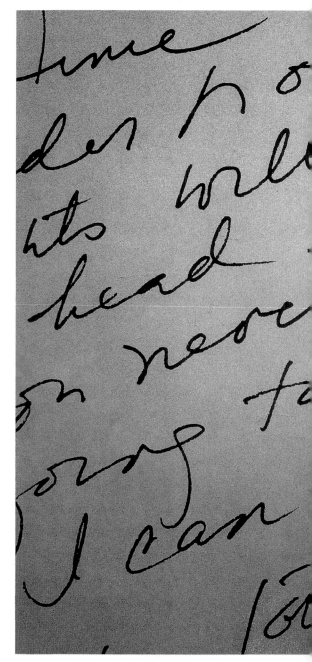

One day do this: a little experiment. Close your doors and sit in your room and just start writing your thoughts – whatsoever comes into your mind.

Don't change them because you need not show this piece of paper to anybody! Just go on writing for ten minutes and then look at them.

This is what your thinking is. If you look at them you will think this is some madman's work. If you show that piece of paper to your most intimate friend he will also look at you and think, "Have you gone crazy?"

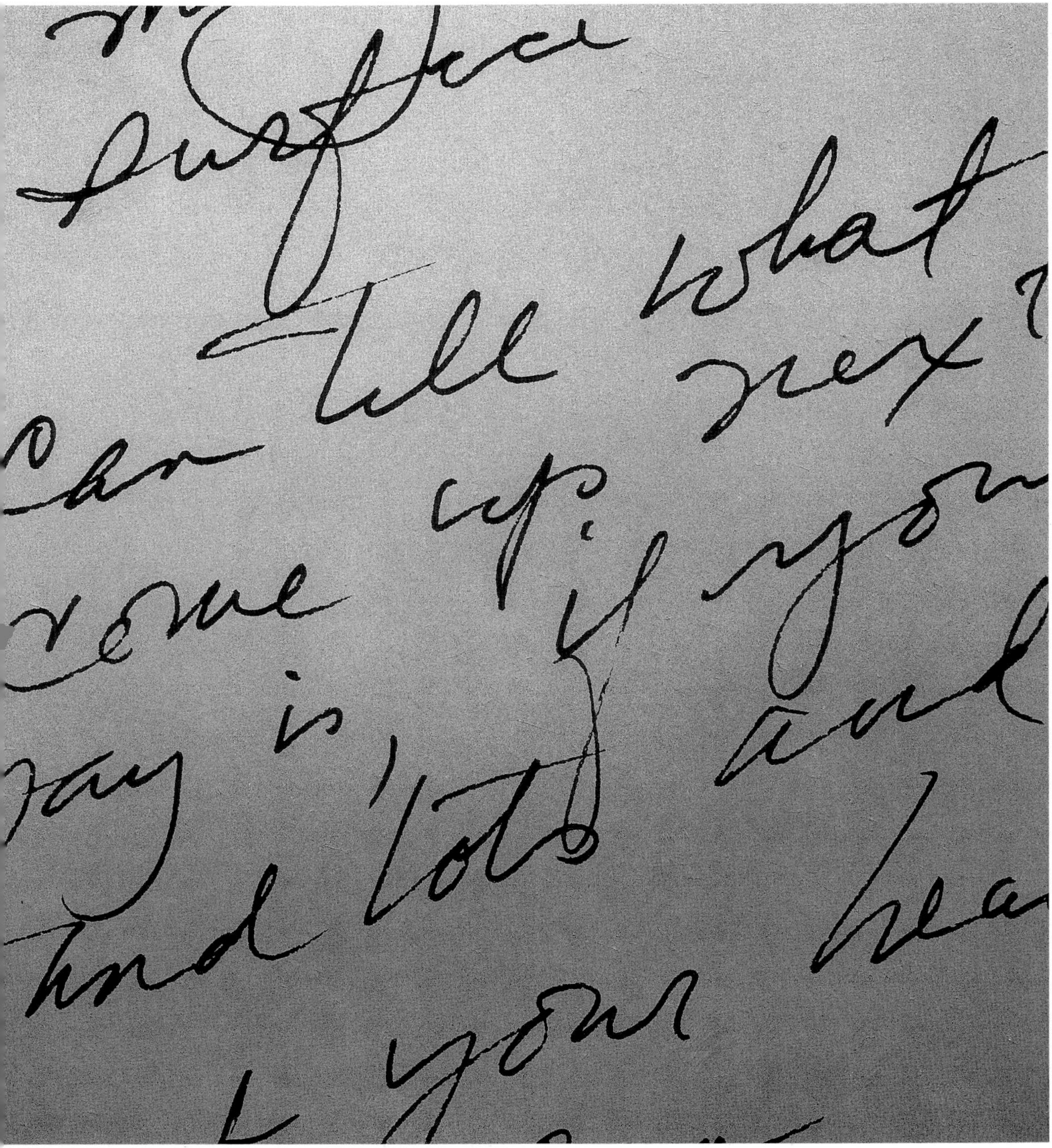

Hand-dancing

A subtle dance enters into your being,
and doors that have remained closed forever start opening.
A new breeze passes through you; dust of centuries is blown away.
You feel as if you have taken a bath, a spiritual bath...

OSHO

Just sit silently and allow your fingers to have their own movement. Feel the movement from the inside. Don't try to see it from the outside, so keep your eyes closed. Let the energy flow more and more into the hands.

The hands are deeply connected with the brain, the right hand with the left side of the brain, the left hand with the right side of the brain. If your fingers can be allowed total freedom of expression many many tensions accumulated in the brain are released. That is the easiest way to release the brain mechanism, its repressions, its unused energy. Your

hands are perfectly capable of doing it. Sometimes you will find the left hand up, sometimes the right hand up. Don't force any pattern, whatsoever is the need of the energy it will take that form. When the left side of the brain wants to release energy, it will take one form. When the right side of the brain is too burdened with energy then there will be a different gesture.

You can become a great meditator through hand gestures. So just sitting silently, play, allow the hands and you will be surprised; it is magical.

Dancing as slow as I can

*Dancing is one of the most beautiful things
that can happen to a man.*

OSHO

...Dancing came into the world as a technique of meditation. In the beginning dancing was not to dance, it was to achieve an ecstasy where the dancer was lost, only the dance remained – no ego, nobody manipulating, the body flowing spontaneously.

There is no need to find any other meditation. Dance itself becomes a meditation if the dancer is lost. The whole point is how to lose oneself. How you do that, or where, is irrelevant. Just lose yourself. A point comes where you are not, and still things go on ... as if you are possessed.

So for at least one hour every day, forget all technique. Make it a point to simply dance to God. So there is no need to be technical – because He is not an examiner. You will simply dance as a small child ... as a prayer. Then dance will have a totally different quality to it. You will feel for the first time that you are taking steps that you have never taken before; that you are moving in dimensions which have never been known to you. Unfamiliar and unknown ground will be traversed.

By and by, as you will become more and more in tune with the unknown, all techniques will disappear. And without techniques, when dance is pure and simple, it is perfect.

Dance as if you are deep in love with the universe, as if you are dancing with your lover. Let God be your lover.

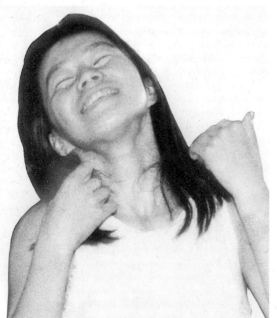

Double dancing

What is the use of meditation?
What do you earn out of it? What is the use of dance?... nothing.
You cannot eat, you cannot drink,
you cannot make a shelter out of dancing.
It seems non-utilitarian.
All that is beautiful and true is non-utilitarian.

OSHO

...Create a small group of friends who can dance together. That will be better, more helpful. Man is so weak that alone it is difficult to continue anything. Hence, schools are needed. So if you are not feeling like doing it one day and others are, their energy moves you. Someday somebody else is not feeling like it but you are, so your energy comes through.

Left alone, man is very weak and will-less. One day you do it and another day you feel that you are tired and have other things to do. Meditations bring results only when they are done in a persistent way. Then it sinks inside you. It is just as if you are digging a hole in the earth. One day you dig in one place, another day in another place. Then you can go on digging for the whole of your life but the well will never be ready. You have to dig in the same place continuously.

So make it a point, at the same time every day. And if it is possible in the same place, very good; the same room, the same atmosphere, burn the same incense ... so the body by and by learns and the mind by and by gets the feel of it. The moment you enter the room you are ready to dance. The room is charged, the time is charged.

Minus-meditation

*It is not possible for you to expose yourself totally
in front of anybody else.
Here in the East we never developed anything like psychoanalysis:
we developed meditation.
That is exposing yourself in front of yourself.
That is the only possibility of being utterly true,
because there is no fear.*

OSHO

Try this method each night for sixty minutes. For forty minutes, just become negative – as negative as you can. Close the doors, put pillows around the room. Unhook the phone, and tell everybody that you are not to be disturbed for one hour. Put a notice on the door saying that for one hour you should be left alone. Make things as dim as possible. Put on some gloomy music, and feel dead. Sit there and feel negative. Repeat "no" as a mantra.

Imagine scenes of the past – when you were very very dull and dead, and you wanted to commit suicide, and there was no zest to life – and exaggerate them. Create the whole situation around you. Your mind will distract you. It will say, "What are you doing? The night is so beautiful, and the moon is full!" Don't listen to the mind. Tell it that it can come later on, but that this time you are devoting completely to negativity.

Be religiously negative. Cry, weep, shout, scream, swear – whatsoever you feel like – but remember one thing: don't become happy, don't allow any happiness. If you catch yourself, immediately give yourself a slap! Bring yourself back to negativity, and start beating the pillows, fighting with them, jumping. Be nasty! And you will find it very very difficult to be negative for these forty minutes.

This is one of the basic laws of the mind – that whatsoever you do consciously, you cannot do. But do it – and when you do it consciously, you will feel a separation. You are doing it but still you are a witness; you are not lost in it. A distance arises, and that distance is tremendously beautiful. But I am not saying to create that distance. That is a by-product – you need not worry about it.

After forty minutes suddenly jump out of the negativity. Throw the pillows away, put on the lights, put on some beautiful music, and have a dance for twenty minutes. Just say "yes! yes! yes!" – let it be your mantra. And then take a good shower. It will uproot all the negativity,

and it will give you a new glimpse of saying yes. And to come to saying yes is what religion is all about. We have been trained to say no – that's how the whole society has become ugly.

So this will cleanse you completely. You have energy, but all around the energy you have negative rocks, and they don't allow it out. Once these rocks are removed you will have a beautiful flow. It is just there, ready to come out, but first you have to go into negativity. Without going deep into the no, nobody can attain to a peak of yes. You have to become a no-sayer, then yea-saying comes out of that.

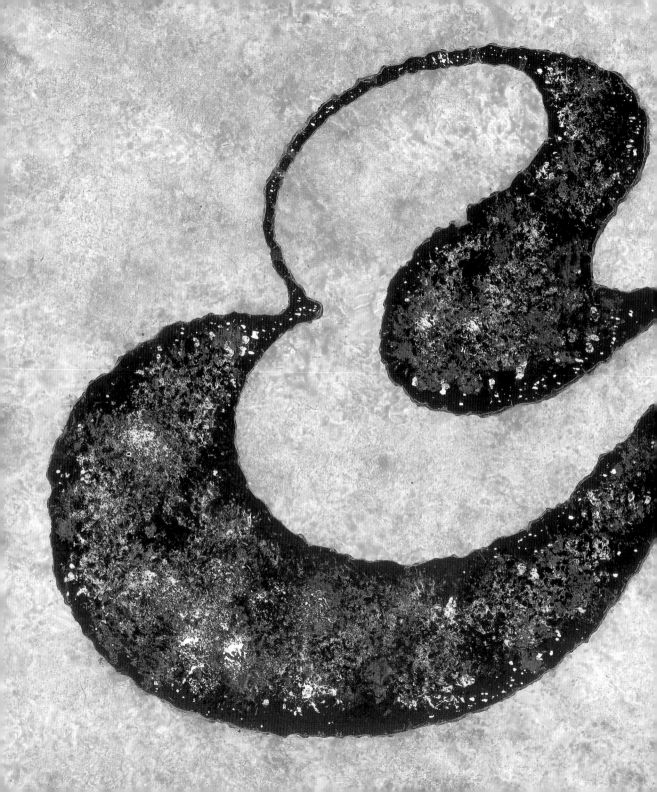

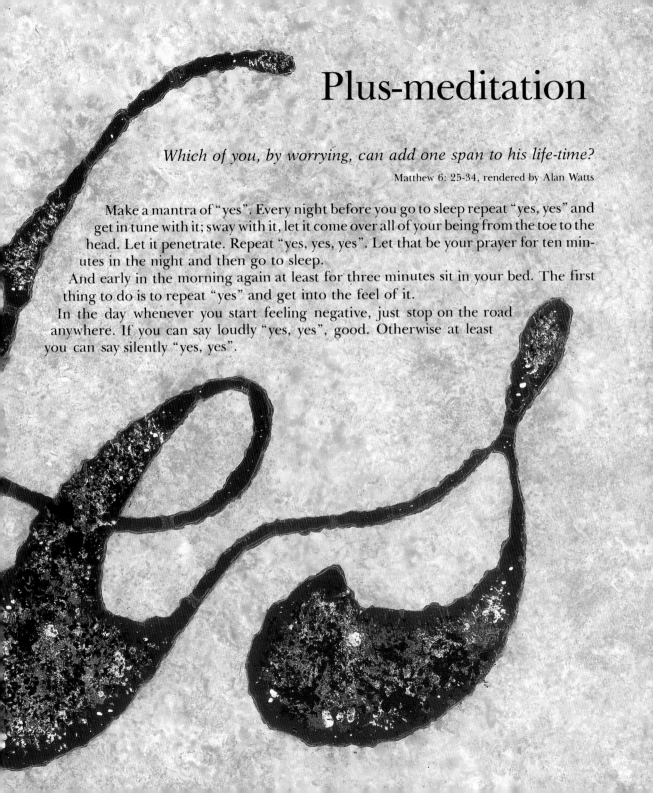

Plus-meditation

Which of you, by worrying, can add one span to his life-time?

Matthew 6: 25-34, rendered by Alan Watts

Make a mantra of "yes". Every night before you go to sleep repeat "yes, yes" and get in tune with it; sway with it, let it come over all of your being from the toe to the head. Let it penetrate. Repeat "yes, yes, yes". Let that be your prayer for ten minutes in the night and then go to sleep.

And early in the morning again at least for three minutes sit in your bed. The first thing to do is to repeat "yes" and get into the feel of it.

In the day whenever you start feeling negative, just stop on the road anywhere. If you can say loudly "yes, yes", good. Otherwise at least you can say silently "yes, yes".

Facing fears

*Face your fears and allow yourself
to unmask their illusion.
Know that you are forever
and that there is nothing
in the unknown that can ever
keep you from happiness and joy.*

Ramtha

Every night for 40 minutes live your fear... Sit in the room, turn the light off and start becoming afraid. Think of all kinds of horrible things, ghosts and demons and whatsoever you can imagine. Create them, imagine that they are dancing around you and trying to grab you for all evil forces. Become really shaken up by your own imagination and go to the extreme of imagination – they are killing you, they are trying to rape you, they are suffocating you. And not one or two – many, on every side they are doing things to you. Get into the fear as deeply as possible and whatsoever happens, go through it.

And the second thing, in the daytime or at any other time, whenever fear arises, accept it. Don't reject it. Don't think that it is something wrong that you have to overcome; it is natural. By accepting it and by expressing it at night, things will start changing.

Taking off the armor

It is easy to see the faults of others,
but difficult to see one's own faults.
One shows the faults of others like chaff winnowed in the wind,
but one conceals one's own faults
as a cunning gambler conceals his dice.

Buddha, *The Dhammapada*

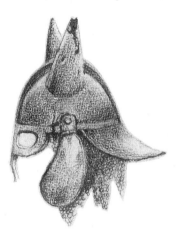

We all know the story pretty well now: living amongst the problems, aggressions and anxieties of our social surroundings, we have to protect ourselves, put on the armor each morning after the cornflakes, because if we don't the spears and arrows of outrageous fortune will pierce us through and through! But at the end of the day, when we are home safe and sound in our own cocoon of security, the armor can come off – theoretically.

Unfortunately sometimes it gets stuck fast and won't unhitch. The straps become knotted and the bolts rusted through constant rainy weather and we end up alone behind the battlements without relief and rest. Try the following for peeling off that tight-fitting armor.

In the night when you go to sleep, take off your clothes, and while taking them off, just imagine that you are not only taking off your clothes, you are taking off your armor too.

Actually do it. Take it off and have a good deep breath – and then go to sleep as if unarmored, with nothing on the body and no restriction.

Cosmic meditation

In the moment that man doubts his immediate impulse, there is no end to complexities.

Alan Watts

Just sitting silently, meditate on the fact that you are boundless, that the boundaries of the universe are your boundaries. Feel expanded, become all-inclusive in that feeling: the sun rises in you, the stars move within you, trees grow and worlds come and disappear – and feel immensely blissful in that expanded state of consciousness...

So whenever you have time and are doing nothing just sit silently and feel expanded. Drop boundaries. Jump out of the boundaries. In the beginning for a few days it will look crazy because we have become too much accustomed to the boundaries. In fact there are no boundaries. The limitation is a mind limitation. Because we believe it to be so, it is.

Feel this oceanic expansion as many times as possible and soon you will start getting in tune with it. Then just a little shift and it is there. Every night when you go to sleep, go with this expanded consciousness. Fall into sleep as if stars are moving within you, the world is coming and disappearing within you. Go to sleep as the universe.

In the morning, in the first moment you become aware that sleep is gone, again remember that expansion and get up out of the bed as the universe. And in the day also, as many times as you can, remember it.

Oh!

What I most want is to spring out of this personality,
Then to sit apart from that leaping.
I've lived too long where I can be reached.

Rumi

Before going to sleep, put off the light, sit on your bed, close your eyes, and exhale deeply through the mouth with the sound "oh". Your stomach goes in, the air moves out, you go on creating the sound "oh". Remember I am not saying "aum", I am simply saying "oh". It will become "aum" automatically; you need not make it "aum". Then it will be false. You simply create the sound "oh".

You will go on relaxing, and your sleep will have a different quality – altogether different. And your sleep has to be changed. Only then can you become more alert and aware...

When you have exhaled completely with your mouth, creating the sound "oh" and you feel now no more exhalation is possible, when the breath has gone out, stop for a single moment. Do not inhale; do not exhale. Stop! In that stop you are the divine. In that stop you are not doing anything, not even breathing. In that stop you are in the ocean. Time is no more there because time moves with the breath. It is as if the whole existence has stopped with you. In that stopping you can become alert about the deepest source of your being and energy. So for a single moment, stop.

Then inhale through the nose. But do not make any effort to inhale. Remember, make all the effort to exhale, but do not make any effort to inhale. Just let the body inhale. You simply relax your hold, and let the body take the inhalation. You do not do anything.

Life breathes by itself; it moves by itself on its own course. It is a river; you unnecessarily go on pushing it. You will see that the body is taking the inhalation. Your effort is not needed, your ego is not needed, you are not needed. You simply become a watcher. You simply see the body taking the inhalation. A deep silence will be felt.

When the body has taken a full inhalation, stop for a single moment again. Then again watch. These two moments are totally different. When you have exhaled completely and stopped, that stopping is just like death. When you have inhaled totally and then stopped, that stopping is the climax of life. Remember, inhalation is equivalent to life, exhalation is equivalent to death.

Feel it! Feel both moments. That is why I tell you to stop twice – once after you have exhaled and again after you have inhaled; so you can feel both life and death. Once you know

that "this" is life, "this" is death, you have transcended both.

The witness is neither death nor life. The witness is never born and never dies. Only the body dies – the mechanism. You have become the third.

Do this meditation for twenty minutes, and then fall down and go to sleep.

Shhh...!

Meditation is your birthright!
It is there, waiting for you to relax a little
so it can sing a song, become a dance.

OSHO

Let silence become your meditation. Whenever you have time, just collapse in silence – and that is exactly what I mean: collapse – as if you are a small child in your mother's womb.

Sit this way and then by and by you will start feeling that you want to put your head on the floor. Then put your head on the floor. Take the womb posture, as the child remains curled up in the mother's womb, and immediately you will feel the silence is coming, the same silence that was there in the mother's womb. Sitting in your bed, go under a blanket and curl up and remain there utterly still, doing nothing.

A few thoughts sometimes will come, let them pass – you just be indifferent, not concerned at all: if they come, good; if they don't come, good. Don't fight, don't push them away. If you fight you will become disturbed, if you push them away, you will become persistent, if you don't want them, they will be very stubborn about going. You simply remain unconcerned, let them be there on the periphery as if traffic noise is there. And it is really a traffic noise, the brain traffic of millions of cells communicating with each other and energy moving and electricity jumping from one cell to another cell. It is just the humming of a great machine, so let it be there.

You become completely indifferent to it, it does not concern you, it is not your problem – somebody else's problem maybe, but not yours. What do you have to do with it? And you will be surprised – moments will come when the noise will disappear, completely disappear, and you will be left all alone.

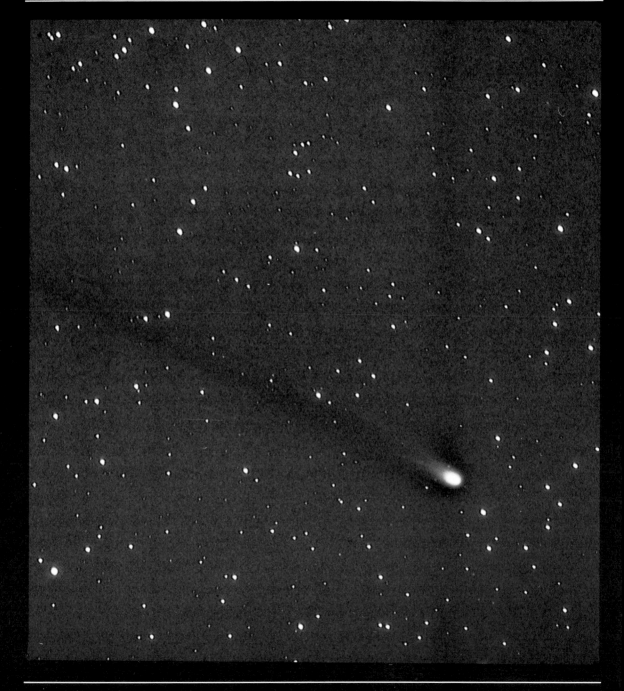

Stars inside

We come into this world alone,
we depart alone
This also is illusion.
I will teach you the way
Not to come, not to go!

Ikkyu

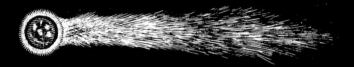

Get more and more in tune with the stars. Whenever there are stars in the night and the night is clear, just lie down on the earth and look at the stars. If you feel attached to a certain star, then concentrate on that. While concentrating on that, think of yourself as being a small lake and that the star is reflected deep inside you. So see the star outside and see it reflected inside you ... and a great joy will arise out of it. Once you get in tune with it you can simply close your eyes and see that star, your star; but first you have to find it.

In the East they have a myth that everybody has a certain star. All those stars are not for everybody, everybody has a particular star. That myth is beautiful.

...You can find one star which belongs to you and to which you belong. There will arise a certain affinity between you and the star because we are made of light, as are the stars. We vibrate as light as do the stars. You can always find a star with which you simply feel in tune, which is on the same wave-length. That is your star; meditate over it.

By and by allow it inside. Look at it, then close your eyes and see it within. Open your eyes; look at it, then close your eyes and see it within. Open your eyes; look at it. Close your eyes; see it within. Open your eyes; look at it. Close your eyes; see it within. Soon you will find it is within you. Then whenever you close your eyes you will find it there.

And when you start feeling it inside, feel it just near the navel; two inches below the navel. Deposit it there; go on depositing it and soon you will feel great light arising inside you as if a star has already in reality burst forth; and it will not be only that you feel it, others will start feeling it – that a certain kind of light has started surrounding your body, your face has become it. Just look for a few nights and you will be able to find your star.

Moon swaying

Full moon.
Quietly awake, you look down
from a corner of the roof,
reminding us it's not time to sleep,
or to drink wine.

Rumi

The next time the full moon is due, start this three days before. Go outside in the open sky, look at the moon and start swaying. Just feel as if you have left everything to the moon – become possessed. Look at the moon, relax and say to it that you are available, and ask the moon to do whatsoever it wants. Then whatsoever happens, allow it.

If you feel like swaying, sway, or if you feel like dancing or singing, do that. But the whole thing should be as if you are possessed – *you* are not the doer – it is just happening. You are just an instrument being played upon.

Do this for the three days before the full moon, and as the moon becomes fuller and fuller you will start feeling more and more energy. You will feel more and more possessed. By the full moon night you will be completely mad. With just one hour's dancing and madness, you will feel relaxed as you have never been before.

Love magic

In a love relationship you should be possessed –
you should not try to possess.
In a love relationship you should surrender;
and you should not go on watching who has the upper hand.

OSHO

Practice love. Sitting alone in your room, be loving. Radiate love. Fill the whole room with your love energy. Feel vibrating with a new frequency, feel swaying as if you are in the ocean of love. Create vibrations of love energy around you. And you will start feeling immediately that something is happening – something in your aura is changing, something around your body is changing; a warmth is arising around your body... You are becoming more alive. Something like sleep is disappearing. Something like awareness is arising. Sway into this ocean. Dance, sing, and let your whole room be filled with love.

In the beginning it feels very weird. When for the first time you can fill your room with love energy, your own energy, which goes on falling and rebouncing on you and makes you so happy, one starts feeling, "Am I hypnotizing myself? Am I deluded? What is happening?" because you have always thought that love comes from somebody else. A mother is needed to love you, a father, a brother, a husband, a wife, a child – but somebody.

Love that depends on somebody is a poor love. Love that is created within you, love that you create out of your own being, is real energy. Then move anywhere with that ocean surrounding you and you will feel that everybody who comes close to you is suddenly under a different kind of energy.

People will look at you with more open eyes. You will be passing them and they will feel that a breeze of some unknown energy has passed them; they will feel fresher. Hold somebody's hand and his whole body will start throbbing. Just be close to somebody and that man will start feeling very happy for no reason at all. You can watch it. Then you are becoming ready to share. Then find a lover, then find a right receptivity for you.

The love-making meditation

This meditation is for lovers who have become somehow stuck in their relationship and the result is that love-making has become too much of a habit – an unhappy habit, or no habit at all!

Just sit facing each other in the night, and hold each other's hands crosswise. For ten minutes look into each other's eyes, and if the body starts moving and swaying, allow it. You can blink the eyes, but go on looking into each other's eyes. If the body starts swaying – it will sway – allow it. Don't let go of each other's hands, whatsoever happens. That should not be forgotten.

After ten minutes, both close the eyes and allow the swaying for ten more minutes. Then stand and sway together, holding hands for ten minutes. This will mix your energy deeply.

A little more melting is needed ... melting into each other.

Let love-making come by itself

Before you move into love, just sit silently together for fifteen minutes holding each other's hands crosswise. Sit in darkness or in a very dim light and feel each other. Get in tune. The way to do that is to breathe together. When you exhale, she exhales; when you inhale, she inhales. Within two to three minutes you can get into it. Breathe as if you are one organism – not two bodies but one. And look into each other's eyes, not with an aggressive look but very softly. Take time to enjoy each other. Play with each other's bodies.

Don't move into love-making unless the moment arises by itself. Not that you make love, but suddenly you find yourself making love. Wait for that. If it does not come, there is no need to force it. It is good. Go to sleep; no need to make love. Wait for that moment for one, two, three days. It will come one day. And

when that moment comes, love will go very deep and it will not create the madness it is creating now. It will be a very very silent, oceanic feeling. But wait for that moment; don't force it.

Love is something which has to be done like meditation. It is something which has to be cherished, tasted very slowly, something that takes you beyond the experience of making love – you are no more there. It is not that you are making love – you are love. Love becomes a bigger energy around you. It transcends you both ... you are both lost in it. But for that you will have to wait.

Wait for the moment and soon you will have the knack of it. Let the energy accumulate and let it happen on its own. By and by, you will become aware when the moment arises. You will start seeing the symptoms of it, the pre-symptoms, and there will be no difficulty.

Love is like God – you cannot manipulate it. It happens when it happens. If it is not happening, there is nothing to be worried about.

ON VACATION

Who sees naught,
Says naught,
Hears naught,
Simply surpasses the Buddha.

Ikkyu

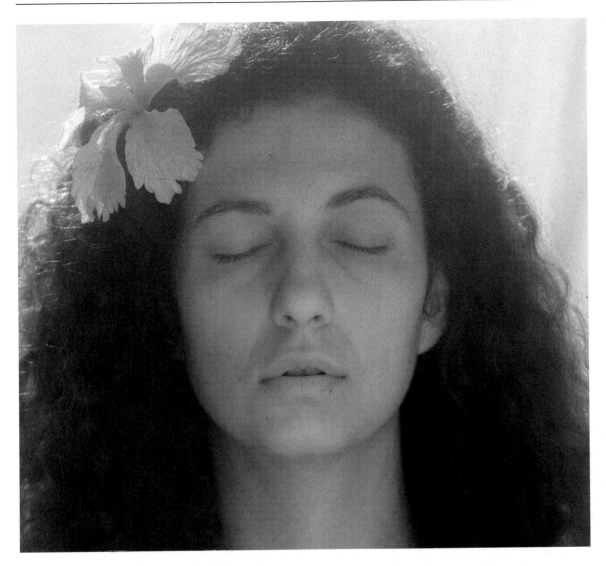

These are a number of techniques that can be tried while traveling or on vacation, when there is more casual time to experiment. The main issue for the over-stressed working person is to find ways to "wind-down" and make the change from work to play.

If the contents of this book are absorbed successfully then the new difference between work and vacation will soon be noticed – it will no longer be so much a matter of winding-down but of remaining at the same level of calm and happiness throughout all activities.

Follow the yes

I can break off from anyone, except that presence within.
Anyone can bring gifts. Give me someone who takes away.

Rumi

For one month follow only the yes, the path that says, "yes". For one month don't follow the path that says "no". Give more cooperation to the yes – that is from where you will become united. No never helps to attain unity. It is always yes that helps, because yes is acceptance, yes is trust, yes is prayer. To be able to say "yes" is to be religious.

The second thing: the no must not be repressed. If you repress it, it will take revenge. If you repress it, it will become more and more powerful and one day will explode and destroy your yes. So never repress the no, just ignore it.

And there is a great difference between repressing and ignoring. You know it is there and you recognize it. You say, "Yes, I know you are there, but I'm going to follow yes." You don't repress it, you don't fight with it, you don't say, "Get out, get lost, I don't want to do anything with you." You don't say anything in anger to it. You don't want to push it away, you don't want to throw it into the basement of your unconsciousness, in the dark mind.

No, you don't do anything to it; you simply recognize that it is there. But you are following the yes, with no grudge, with no complaint, with no anger. Simply follow yes, not taking any attitude about no. Ignoring it is the greatest art to kill no. If you fight with it you have already become a victim, a very subtle victim; the no has already won over you. When you fight with no you have said "no" to no. That is how it has taken possession of you from the back door. Don't say, "no" even to no – just ignore it.

For one month follow yes and don't fight with no. You will be surprised that by and by it becomes lean and thin because it is becoming starved, and one day suddenly you see it is no more there. And when it is no more there, all the energy involved in it is released and that released energy will make your yes a great stream.

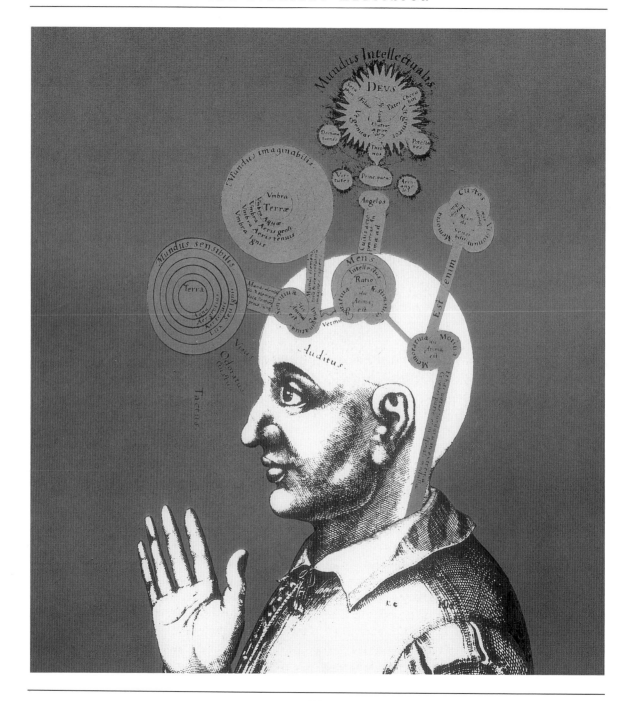

I am not this

An enemy can hurt an enemy,
and man who hates can harm another man;
but a man's own mind, if wrongly directed,
can do him far greater harm.

Buddha, *The Dhammapada*

Mind is rubbish! It is not that you have rubbish and somebody else hasn't. It is rubbish, and if you go on bringing rubbish out, you can go on and on; you can never bring it to a point where it ends. It is self-perpetuating rubbish, so it is not dead, it is dynamic. It grows and has life of its own. So if you cut it, leaves will sprout again.

Bringing it out doesn't mean that you will become empty. It will only make you aware that this mind that you thought is you, with which you have been identified up to now, is not you. Bringing it up, you will become aware of the separation, the gulf, between you and it. The rubbish remains but you are not identified with it, that's all. You become separate, you know you are separate.

So you have only to do one thing: don't try to fight with the rubbish, and don't try to change it. Simply watch, and just remember one thing, "I am not this." Let this be the mantra: "I am not this." Remember it, and become alert and see what happens. There is a change immediately. The rubbish will be there, but it is no longer a part of you. That remembrance becomes a renunciation of it.

Cut off your head

*The mystic experience
is an extraordinary one
because it is not
an intellectual experience.*

U.G. Krishnamurti

This is one of the most intriguing Tantra meditations. It has to be experienced!

Walk and think that the head is no more there, just the body. Sit and think that the head is no more there, just the body. Continuously remember that the head is nowhere. Visualize yourself without the head. Have a picture of yourself enlarged without the head; look at it. Let your mirror be lowered in the bathroom so when you see, you cannot see your head, just the body.

A few days of remembrance and you will feel such weightlessness happening to you, such tremendous silence, because it is the head that is the problem. If you can conceive of yourself as headless – and that can be conceived, there is no trouble in it – then more and more you will be centered in the heart.

Just at this very moment you can visualize yourself headless. Then you will understand what I am saying immediately.

Running on empty

Again, I'm within my self.
I walked away, but here I come sailing back, feet in the air,
upside-down, as a saint when he opens his eyes from prayer:
Now. The room, the tablecloth, familiar faces.

Rumi

Make it a point every night before you go to sleep to close your eyes and for twenty minutes go into your emptiness. Accept it, let it be there. Fear arises – let that be there too.
Tremble with fear but don't reject this space that is being born there.

Within two or three weeks you will be able to feel its beauty, you will be
able to feel its benediction. Once you have touched that benediction,
fear will disappear of its own accord. You are not to fight with it.

Within three weeks one day suddenly you will see such
blessings arising, such an upsurge of energy, such a joyous quality to your being, as if the night is over and
the sun has come on the horizon.

The naked earth

Meditation is your intrinsic nature
– it is you.
It has nothing to do
with your doings:
you cannot have it,
you cannot not have it,
it cannot be possessed,
it is not a thing, it is you.

OSHO

Sometime try a small experiment: just naked stand somewhere, on the beach, near the river – just naked in the sun – and start jumping, jogging, and feel your energy is flowing through your feet, through your legs to the earth.

Jog and feel your energy is going through your legs into the earth; then after a few minutes of jogging, just stand silently rooted to the earth and just feel a communion of your feet with the earth. Suddenly you will feel very, very rooted, grounded solid. You will see the earth communicates, you will see your feet communicate. A dialogue arises between the earth and you.

Befriend a tree

There is no illusion, no deception when there is no desire,
conscious or unconscious, for any experience of the kind,
when one's wholly indifferent to the coming and going
of all experience, when one is not asking for anything.

J. Krishnamurti

Go to a tree, talk to the tree, touch the tree, embrace the tree, feel the tree, just sit by the side of the tree, let the tree feel that you are a good man and that you are not in the mood to harm.

By and by friendship arises and you will start feeling that when you come, the quality of the tree immediately changes. You will feel it, on the bark of the tree you will feel tremendous energy moving when you come. When you touch the tree, she is as happy as a child, as a beloved. When you sit by the tree, you will feel many things, and soon you will be able to feel that if you are sad and come to the tree,

your sadness will disappear just in the presence of the tree.

Then only will you be able to understand that you are interdependent. You can make the tree happy, and the tree can make you happy, and the whole of life is interdependent. This interdependence I call God.

Dancing like a tree

The sun is love.
The lover, a speck circling the sun.
A Spring wind moves to dance
any branch that isn't dead.

Rumi

Just raise your hands and feel like a tree in a strong wind. Dance like a tree in the rains and the winds. Let your whole energy become a dancing energy, sway and move with the wind, just feel the wind passing through you. Forget that you have a human body – you are a tree, get identified with the tree.

Go into the open if it is possible, stand amongst the trees, become a tree and let the wind pass through you. To feel identified with a tree is immensely strengthening, nourishing. One easily enters into the primal consciousness. Trees are still there; talk with trees, hug the trees and you will suddenly feel that everything is back. And if it is not possible to go out then just stand in the middle of the room, visualize yourself as being a tree and start dancing.

Flying high

I am not saying meditation will solve life problems.
I am simply saying that, if you are in a meditative state,
problems will disappear, not be solved.
There is no need to solve a problem.
In the first place the problem is created by a tense mind.

OSHO

You cannot find a better situation to meditate than while flying at a high altitude. The higher the altitude, the easier is the meditation. Hence, for centuries, meditators have been moving to the Himalayas to find a high altitude.

When the gravitation is less and the earth is very far away, many pulls of the earth are far away. You are far away from the corrupted society that man has built. You are surrounded by clouds and the stars and the moon and the sun and the vast space... So do one thing: start feeling one with that vastness, and do it in three steps.

The first step is: for a few minutes just think that you are becoming bigger ... you are filling the whole plane.

Then the second step: start feeling that you are becoming even bigger, bigger than the plane, in fact the plane is now inside you.

And the third step: feel that you have expanded into the whole sky... Now these clouds that are moving, and the moon and the stars – they are moving in you: you are huge, unlimited.

This feeling will become your meditation, and you will feel completely relaxed and non-tense.

Color blue

God only knows, I don't,
what keeps me laughing.
The stem of a flower
moves when the air moves.

Rumi

Whenever you have some view of something blue, the blue of the sky, the blue of the river just sit silently and look into the blue of it and you will feel a very deep tuning with it. A great silence will descend on you whenever you meditate on the color blue.

Blue is one of the most spiritual colors because it is the color of silence, stillness. It is the color of tranquillity, rest, relaxation. So whenever you are really relaxed, inside you will suddenly feel a blue luminosity. And if you can feel a blue luminosity you will immediately feel relaxed. It works both ways.

Sky blue

Meditation is adventure,
the greatest adventure
the human mind can undertake.
Meditation is just to be,
not doing anything – no action,
no thought, no emotion.
You just are and it is a sheer delight.
From where does this delight come
when you are not doing anything?
It comes from nowhere,
or it comes from everywhere.
It is uncaused, because the existence
is made of the stuff called joy.

OSHO

Meditate on the sky and whenever you have time just lie down on the ground; look at the sky. Let that be your contemplation. If you want to pray, pray to the sky. If you want to meditate, meditate on the sky, sometimes with open eyes, sometimes with closed eyes. Because the sky is within too; as it is big without, within it is the same.

We are just standing on the threshold of the inner sky and the outer sky and they are exactly proportionate. As the outside sky is infinite, so is the inner sky. We are just standing on the threshold, either way you can be dissolved. And these are the two ways to dissolve.

If you dissolve in the outside sky then it is prayer, if you dissolve into the inside sky then it is meditation.

Flower-fragrance

Those on the way are almost invisible to those who are not.
A man or a woman recognizes God and starts out.
The others say he, or she, is losing faith.

Rumi

Be near a flower, let the smell fill you. Then by and by move away from the flower very slowly but continue being attentive to the smell, the fragrance. As you move away the fragrance will become more and more subtle and you will need more awareness to feel it. Become the nose. Forget about the whole body and bring all the energy to the nose as if only the nose exists. If you lose track of the smell, go a few steps further ahead, again catch hold of the smell, then move back...

By and by you will be able to smell a flower from a very, very great distance. Nobody else will be able to smell that flower from there. Then go on moving in a very subtle way – you are making the object subtle. And then a moment will come when you will not be able to smell the smell. Now smell the absence of where the fragrance was just a moment before. It is no longer there. That is the other part of its being – the absent part, the dark part. If you can smell the absence of the smell, if you can feel that it makes a difference, it makes a difference. Then the object has become very subtle. Now it is reaching near to the no-thought state of samadhi.

Wake up shake

Rub your eyes and be awake.

Mikhail Naimy, *The Book of Mirdad*

Stop thinking.

And whenever you find yourself thinking, catch hold of yourself, and give a good jerk to the head – a real jerk so that everything inside goes upside down. Make it a constant habit, and within a few weeks you will see that that jerk helps. Suddenly you become more aware.

In Zen monasteries, the master moves around with a staff, and whenever he sees some disciple dozing, thinking, and with dreams floating on the face, he will immediately hit him hard on the head. It goes like a shock through the spine, and in a split second, thinking stops, and suddenly awareness arises.

I cannot follow you with a staff. You give yourself a jerk, a good one, and even if people think you are a little mad don't be worried. There is only one madness, and that is of the mind. Too much thinking is the only madness. Everything else is beautiful. Mind is the disease.

Voice energy

Except it have a meaning a word is but an echo in the void.

Mikhail Naimy, *The Book of Mirdad*

When meditation releases energy in you, it will find all sorts of ways to be expressed. It depends on what type of talent you have. If you are a painter and meditation releases energy, you will paint more, you will paint madly, you will forget everything, the whole world. Your whole energy will be brought into painting. If you are a dancer, your meditation will make you a very deep dancer. It depends on the capacity, talent, individuality, personality. So nobody knows what will happen. Sometimes sudden changes will happen. A person who was very silent, who was never talkative, suddenly becomes talkative. It may have been repressed, he may not have been ever allowed to talk. When the energy arises and flows, he may start talking.

Every night before you go to sleep, for forty minutes sit facing the wall and start talking – talk loudly. Enjoy it ... be with it. If you find that there are two voices, then talk from both of the sides. Give your support to this side, then answer from the other side, and see how you can create a beautiful dialogue.

Don't try to manipulate it; because you are not saying it for anybody. If it is going to be crazy, let it be. Don't try to cut anything or censor anything, because then the whole point is lost. Do it for at least ten days. Just put your whole energy into it.

PART OF THE GAME

The mind cannot become the Buddha;
The body cannot become the Buddha;
Only what cannot become the Buddha
Can become the Buddha.

Ikkyu

There are various well-tried methods which come with the acceptance of meditation: methods which enhance the changes that naturally occur in life when meditation is a part of it.

Many of the modern proponents of the "new age" will assert that the gathering of spiritual understanding is somehow something to do with a vague thing called the "soul." The soul is a little like the traditional image of God – it exists somewhere "up there," perhaps in the sky, perhaps in heaven – nobody quite seems to know.

Meditation is in the body – it is physiological – it affects the body and the mind-brain. You will notice the difference within and around your body so for all purposes it is much simpler to regard the body when changing your life in this way, the spirit and the mind are somewhat less tangible.

A physiological understanding of meditation and its attendant methods is also happier in the sense that we can more easily appreciate what we are doing if we relate it to the body. Start thinking in terms of psychology and spirituality and the picture becomes muddied through lack of information, particularly in this era of esoteric secrecy.

So, the following are some very down-to-earth methods that will be applicable if you want to enhance your meditations.

Breathing

When the breath wanders, the mind is unsteady, but when the breath is still, so is the mind still.

Hatha Yoga Pradipika

Breathing is life. Breathing is an intrisic part of your life. It is going to be there always, until you die. One cannot do without it. It changes with our emotions and moods: becomes short and shallow when we are angry; deep and faster when we make love; slow and abundant when we are happy; and almost disappears when we are afraid. It is a miraculous tool.

Down the ages breathing has been used as a tool by hundreds of Masters all around the world. Some techniques, like in yoga, use breathing to steady the emotions, revitalize the body and clarify the mind. Others, like in Dynamic meditation, use breathing to trigger the emotions in order to express them and get free and more detached from them. There is no right or wrong. All these techniques can be of immense value if used at the right time.

For example, if you feel depressed, going into Vipassana will only suppress the emotions you are already suppressing and will simply make things worse. In that case Dynamic meditation would be good for you. But if you feel happy and clear and you want to go deeper into meditation, Vipassana is the one for you. The ground rule should be that if a technique makes you feel more energetic, more silent, more happy, more laughing, more relaxed then it is good for you. If it makes you feel tense, tired, depressed and more serious, then you need to move to another technique.

But breathing isn't just there while we are meditating. It is with us all the time. And it can be used as a tool not only when we are following this or that technique, but during our everyday life, every moment.

Most of us are not even in touch with our breathing. We take it for granted. Our breathing is shallow, in fact we are not really breathing, we are not taking the breath – life – fully. So the first thing is to become again in touch with the breath. Watch as it changes with your moods, don't try to change it or do anything with it, you need only to get to know it. Notice what happens when you become sad or excited, notice how it changes when you relax again.

When you feel more familiar with your breath try this little exercise. It will bring freshness to your mind and body, both in the morning, when you go to work, and in the evening when you come back from it. It will also give you an insight into how easy it is to relax through breathing. It thus becomes an extremely precious tool for you to use whenever the need arises.

Whenever you find time, just for a few minutes relax the breathing system, nothing else – there is no need to relax the whole body. Sitting in the train or plane, or in the car, nobody will become aware that you are doing something. Just relax the breathing system. Let it be as when it is functioning naturally. Then close your eyes and watch the breathing going in, coming out, going in.

Don't concentrate. If you concentrate, you create trouble, because then everything becomes a disturbance. If you try to concentrate sitting in the car, then the noise of the car becomes a disturbance, the person sitting beside you becomes a disturbance.

Meditation is not concentration. It is simple awareness. You simply relax and watch the breathing. In that watching, nothing is excluded. The car is humming – perfectly okay, accept it. The traffic is passing – that's okay, part of life. The fellow passenger snoring by your side, accept it. Nothing is rejected.

Once breathing becomes something more conscious there are many places it can be directed. Any situation which requires careful awareness of the body, the people around the body and the situations that arise from contact with the world, can be helped into being happier and healthier by conscious breathing.

Take for example the conditions of dealing with problems of anger or pain or relationships. Breathing consciously through the part of the body which feels most affected by such conditions will help to deal with them. Practice by directing your breathing to different parts of the body.

Atisha, a Tibetan Master, developed a very beautiful method: when you breathe in, breathe in all the misery and suffering of all the beings of the world – past, present and future. And when you breathe out, breathe out all the joy that you have, all the blissfulness that you have, all the benediction that you have. Breathe out, pour yourself into existence. This is the method of compassion: drink in all the suffering and pour out all the blessings.

And you will be surprised if you do it. The moment you take all the sufferings of the world inside you, they are no longer sufferings. The heart immediately transforms the energy. The heart is a transforming force: drink in misery, and it is transformed into blissfulness...then pour it out.

Once you have learned that your heart can do this magic, this miracle, you would like to do it again and again. Try it. It is one of the most practical methods – simple, and it brings immediate results. Do it today, and see.

Cleansing

Lying back in this presence, no longer able to eat or drink,
I float freely like a corpse in the ocean.

Rimu

Down the ages monks and yogis practiced fasting, dieting and other type of body cleansing routines. Unfortunately these routines were performed as punishment, as means to get a better place in heaven or as countdowns towards enlightenment. These methods need to be used carefully, as they are not a means unto themselves. If used on their own, they not only go against meditation but can even be quite dangerous.

Since the subject of fasting is a constant issue,

we are mentioning it in this book, although fasting is not necessary to enhance meditation, in fact Bhagwan Shree Rajneesh is absolutely against it. It can at the most make you feel good in your body. You can experiment with it but don't overdo it.

There are a few basic decisions to be made before embarking on a fast. Fasting is not quite like dieting. We generally have difficulties with dieting! One might imagine that as fasting is one step "more" than dieting, that it is therefore that much "more" difficult. This is not necessarily the case, for with dieting we are generally asked by those who provide the diets to eat different types and quantities of foods that perhaps do not appeal to us and therefore the temptation for what does appeal to us still exists. Fasting is a technique which cleans the body of food altogether and the physiological and psychological changes are different.

So, first decide how long you are going to fast for. The maximum should be four days as anything longer requires medical supervision. Choose a time when you are not busy or under stress as the changes in the body can be quite considerable during a fast. Also, you should not be taking any medication during a fast so do not choose to fast during illness or if you are taking any kind of drug or medication.

Decide next what kind of fast you are going to do – whether it be a grape fast, a fruit fast, a liquid fast or a vegetable juice fast. Once decided you must stick to that fast and not change the content of it during the fast.

Drink at least five glasses of natural mineral water each day and better still seven or eight glasses. With a fruit juice or vegetable juice fast, drink the same amount but try "chewing" the juice instead of swallowing it straight down.

The first three days of the fast are the most difficult because the body is working to rid itself of impurities. It is important at this time to help your body eliminate wastes by using a mild natural laxative or an enema. As these toxins are released you may also experience bad breath; headaches; a coated tongue or even vomiting. If you are doing a water fast and experience palpitations, change to fruit juice and to fruit if you are on a juice fast. Breathing problems may also occur and if they or the palpitations persist, break the fast slowly.

Since fasting slows down the circulation you probably want to wear warm clothes, and you might find yourself feeling dizzy if you move too quickly or suddenly. It is suggested to take walks in nature or do any other light physical exercise while fasting, but avoid any strenuous activity. Once your mind stops sending your stomach the message that it is craving food you will be able to experience the greatest benefit of fasting which is simply feeling an increased awareness of your senses.

George Bernard Shaw has said that any fool can go on a fast but it takes a wise man to break it properly. The first time you taste food again your mind will tell you to eat like crazy. You must re-accustom your body slowly to eating, choosing your first food with care. Break your fast in the evening and do not eat again until this food has completely passed through your system. Vegetarians should take about a pound of fresh fruit – grapes (without seeds), or other juicy fruits, but not apples, bananas or citrus fruits. Those with a heavier diet, such as meat-eaters, should have the same amount of steamed vegetables. Gradually add salads, light grains and vegetables until you return to your usual diet. Alcohol, coffee, tea and seasoning should be avoided while breaking a fast.

Music

*If you love music, you love it only because
around it somehow you feel meditation happening.*

OSHO

Music creates such a harmony that even God starts nodding at you, saying yes to you, suddenly the sky starts touching you; you are overwhelmed by the beyond. And when the beyond is close to you, when the footsteps of the beyond are heard, something inside you gets the challenge, becomes silent, quieter, calmer, cool, collected.

Music is meditation – meditation crystallized in a certain dimension. Meditation is music – music melting into the dimensionless. They are not two.

If you love music, you love it only because around it somehow you feel meditation happening. You are absorbed by it, you become drunk in it. Something of the unknown starts descending around you... God starts whispering. Your heart beats in a different rhythm, one in tune with the universe. Suddenly you are in a deep orgasm with the whole. A subtle dance enters into you and doors that have remained closed forever start opening. A new breeze passes through you; dust of the centuries is blown away. You feel as if you have taken a bath, a spiritual bath; you have been under a shower – clean, fresh, virgin.

Music is meditation, meditation is music. These are two doors to approach the same phenomenon.

Because music and meditation are so much part of each other, the active meditations have been designed with music. The music will enhance the

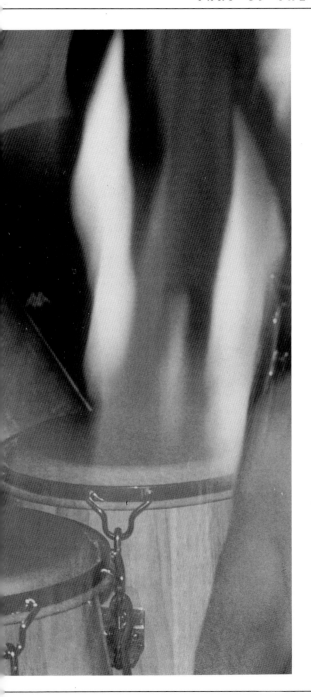

meditation as well as telling you – when the music changes or stops – when to move onto the next step of the meditation.

Tapes have been recorded specially for the active meditations, included or not included in them: the silent part of the meditation. If you are interested in doing one or a few of the active meditations contact any of these distribution centers for purchasing the tapes:

United States: Chidvilas, P.O. Box 17550, Boulder, CO 80308, Tel: (303)665 6611 or (800)777 7743.

United Kingdom: Purnima Rajneesh Publications, Spring House, Spring Place, London NW5 3BH, Tel: (01)284 1415.

The Whirling meditation is a technique invented by the Sufis, the mystics of Persia. The Sufis love music and singing and have many musical tapes in New Age book stores. Use this opportunity to buy yourself a nice set of tapes to play during the Whirling meditation. You can play different pieces each time or if you want to whirl for a longer time, just put the tape on and listen to a whole side.

During the crying part of the Mystic Rose some dramatic or melancholic music will help, for example *L'Adaggio di Albinoni* or Gregorian chants. But crying can also be triggered by a very beautiful music, like the *Canon D* of Pachabel, which brings you into your heart. Anything that makes tears roll down can be played during this stage of the meditation. A special tape is also available for this meditation.

Use music in your meditations or as a meditation, listen to it whole-heartedly, feel the rhythm, the melody, absorb it and you will feel a tremendous joy arise in you, a deep silence. This is meditation.

Sounds

*Meditation is neither a journey in space
nor a journey in time, but an instantaneous awakening.*

J. Krishnamurti

Every culture and society from time immemorial has conceived of sound as a form of power, magic or healing. The witches of the Dark Ages used spells and incantations, and indeed they are still used today. The Welsh sing! The people of the ancient East created mantras.

If you have a musical ear, if you have a heart which can understand music – not only understand but feel – then a mantra will be helpful, because then you can become one with the inner sounds, then you can move with those sounds to more and more subtle layers. Then a moment comes when all sounds stop and only the universal sound remains. That is *aum*.

Mantras are Sanskrit syllables, words or phrases designed to heal and bring a higher state of consciousness when used in meditation. At their most fundamental level they have existed forever in the cosmos – basic sounds that cannot be destroyed.

There are said to be five basic qualities within all true mantras. They are: the mantra was originally revealed to and handed down by a sage who attained self-realization through it; it has a certain meter and a presiding deity; it has a *bija* or seed at its essence which invests it with special power; it has divine cosmic energy or *shakti*; and, it has a key which must be unlocked through constant repetition before pure consciousness is revealed. The idea is that the energy manifests itself through the sound, making a specific effect on the body and the awareness. By practicing for a long time, the sound vibration will have its effect.

The mantras used in the chart are guidelines, you can either pick the one that sounds good to you or make up your own. Any sound which feels aesthetic and beautiful, any sound which creates a thrill and joy in the heart, will do. Even if it doesn't belong to any language, that is not the point at all – you can find just pure sounds that are even more deep-going. Because when you use a certain word, it has a certain meaning – those meanings create

SANSKRIT	PRONUNCIATION	PROPERTIES
ORIGINAL MANTRA		
Om	ohm	The original Mantra The root of all sounds and letters
TIBETAN MANTRAS		
Om Mani Padmi Hum	ohm mah-nee pah-dmee hum	Develops the compassion of the enlightened beings
Om Muni Muni Mahamuni Shakyiamuni Soha	ohm mooh-nee mooh-nee mah-ha-mooh-nee sha-kia-mooh-nee so-huh	Healing
Om Vajra Sattva Uh	ohm vah-jrah saht-vuh hum	Purifies all past and present negativity
Om Ah Hum	ohm ah hum	Purifies body, word and mind
Om Tare Tutare Ture Soha	ohm tah-reh too-tah-reh too-reh so-huh	Brings inspiration and fortune to ones goals.
INDIAN MANTRAS		
Ram	rahm	Brings truth, righteousness and virtue Male aspect
Sita	see-tah	Female aspect of Ram When repeated with Ram as Sitaram, embodies the energy of perfect union
Shyam	shyahm	Transmutes all emotions into unconditional love Male aspect
Radha	rah-duh	Female aspect of Shyam
Om Namah Sivaya	ohm-nuh-muh shivai-uh	Purifies and destroys all negativity
Om Namo Narayanaya	ohm nuh-mo nah-rai-uh-nai-uh	Brings strength and helps regain harmony in times of trouble
Om Aim Saraswatyai Namah	ohm aym suh-ruh-swht-yai nuh-muh-huh	Promotes creativity and wisdom
Soham	soh-hum	Means "I am That" Unifies with the Absolute

limitation. When you use a pure sound, it has no limitation, it is infinite.

You can repeat your mantra aloud, in a whisper, or silently. The important thing is to feel the vibration of the mantra all over the body, from the feet to the head, from the head to the feet. Each repetition of the mantra falls into your consciousness like a rock thrown into a pool and ripples arise and spread to the very end. The ripples go on expanding and touch the whole body.

Doing this there will be moments – and they will be the most beautiful moments – when you will not be repeating and everything has stopped. Enjoy it. If thoughts start coming, again start repeating.

You can find your own pace. After two or three days you will find what suits you. To a few people a very fast, almost overlapping repetition, suits them. To others very slowly is more suitable, so it depends on you. But whatsoever feels good, continue.

If you feel more in tune with pure sounds than words, humming can be very satisfying. You simply close your mouth lightly and hum a low and deep sound, keeping the same note all the way through.

Humming can be a tremendous help and you can do it whenever... At least once a day, if you can do it twice, it will be good. It is such a great inner music that it brings peace to your whole being; then your conflicting parts start falling in tune and by and by a subtle music which you can hear arises in your body. After three or four months you will be just sitting silently and you can hear a subtle music, a harmony inside, a kind of humming. Everything is functioning so perfectly well, like a perfectly functioning car whose engine is humming.

A good driver knows when something goes wrong. The passengers may not become alert but the good driver knows immediately when the humming changes. Then the humming is no more harmonious. A new noise is coming. Nobody else is aware, but one who loves driving will immediately become aware that something is going wrong. The engine is not functioning as it should.

A good hummer by and by starts feeling when things are going wrong. If you have eaten too much you will find your inner harmony is missing and by and by you will have to choose: either eat too much or have the inner harmony. And the inner harmony is so precious, so divine, such a bliss, who bothers to eat more?

And without any effort to diet you find you are eating in a more balanced way. Then the humming goes still deeper, you will be able to see which foods disturb your humming; you eat something heavy and it stays too long in the system and the humming is not so perfect.

Once humming starts you will find when sex is rising, when it is not rising, and if the wife and husband are both humming you will be surprised how great a harmony arises between two persons and how by and by they become intuitive, how they start feeling when the other is feeling sad. There is no need to say; when the husband is tired the wife knows it instinctively because they both function upon the one wavelength.

ACTIVE MEDITATIONS

What is Tao?
A huge tree grows from a tiny sprout,
a nine-storey tower rises from a heap of earth,
a thousand-mile journey begins from one's feet.

Lao Tzu, *Tao Te Ching*

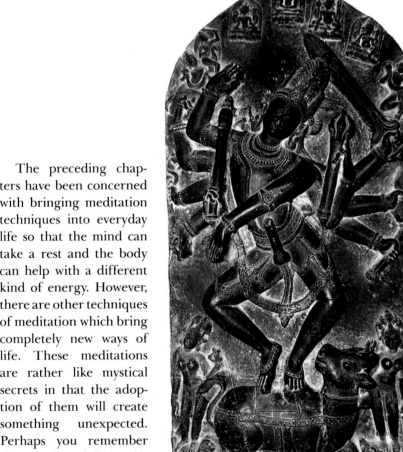

The preceding chapters have been concerned with bringing meditation techniques into everyday life so that the mind can take a rest and the body can help with a different kind of energy. However, there are other techniques of meditation which bring completely new ways of life. These meditations are rather like mystical secrets in that the adoption of them will create something unexpected. Perhaps you remember the mention of this at the very beginning in the introduction to the book. This following section will provide the most dramatic results of all.

Also, these techniques cannot so easily be accommodated within ordinary living conditions – they need a special time and place – in fact they might be called the advanced class.

Look at these techniques with care – use them slowly – i.e. to begin with do not go crazy to be an advanced pupil – a little at a time and the result will be better.

They can all be done alone, but the energy will be more powerful if they are done in a group. It is an individual experience so you should remain oblivious of others around you. Wear loose clothing, specially around the waist: you need to feel comfortable while doing any of these meditations. Not all of them need to be done on an empty stomach, though it is advisable not to eat too much or right before the meditation. Choose a comfortable place where you will not be disturbed and where you will not disturb others during the meditation.

If unpleasant physical symptoms persist for more than three days doing any of these techniques, discontinue and check with you doctor.

Dynamic

A woodcutter, a stone-breaker need not do cathartic meditation –
the whole day they are doing it.
But for the modern man things have changed.

Bhagwan Shree Rajneesh

First stage: ten minutes (above and left)
Breathing rapidly in and out through the nose, concentrate always on the exhalation. The breath should move deeply into the lungs, and the chest expands with each inhalation. Be as fast as you can in your breathing, making sure breathing stays deep. Do this as totally as you possibly can; without tightening up your body, make sure neck and shoulders stays relaxed. Continue on, until you literally become the breathing, allowing breath to be chaotic (that means not in a steady, predictable way). Once your energy is moving, it will begin to move your body. Allow these body movements to be there, use them to help you build up even more energy. Moving your arms and body in a natural way will help your energy to rise. Feel your energy building up; don't let go during the first stage and never slow down.

Dynamic meditation is really something! At the beginning of the book and at the beginning of this section we mentioned that certain meditations are more powerful than others – this one is perhaps the most powerful of them all. Watch out!

This meditation has been designed to let loose the old, stale, repressed emotions stored in the body. By releasing that energy one is able to feel more alive, more energetic and enjoy life more fully. Try it first for 20 days, this is the minimum if you want to experience a deep change, and then for longer if you want a real transformation.

Anger, frustration, deep sadness, fear, insecurity are feelings most often brought out by the Dynamic. It is not that the meditation creates those feelings, they have always been there inside you, they have prevented you from enjoying your life. In fact these feelings are the very cause of your misery, tension, dullness. Once you start opening the valve, everything comes out in an explosion. This is why the process of releasing emotions should be carried through until you start feeling a stillness inside.

After the first day of Dynamic you will experience many muscle aches. This is perfectly normal as you are using muscles you have not used for a long time.

Second stage: ten minutes (above)
Explode! Let go of everything that needs to be
thrown out. Go totally mad, scream, shout, cry,
jump, shake, dance, sing, laugh, throw yourself
around. Hold nothing back, keep your whole body
moving. A little acting often helps to get you started.
Never allow your mind to interfere with what is
happening. Be total.

Do Dynamic on an empty stomach, at sunrise
when possible, but otherwise any time of the day
that suits you is fine. It is important to keep your
eyes closed throughout or wear a blindfold, as
opening your eyes would dissipate the energy.

The hard and fast breathing performed in the
first stage will bring oxygen into the body and
energize every part. The heart will be pumping
blood into the blood stream a lot faster than usual.
The energy caused by this bodily process will build
up to a climax.

In the second stage you totally let go. This is
your opportunity to cathart – to throw out all the
poison that has accumulated in you.

In the third stage you come back to your center.
The sound "hoo" hits at the very center of your

being and it grounds you. There is a variation of
the third stage of this meditation for those who
suffer from bad backs or are handicapped in some
way: instead of jumping, move your pelvis back,
and forth as you push out the sound. The effect is
not as strong, but it is better to find another way of
doing the meditation than not to do it at all.

Naturally by the time the fourth stage arrives a
stillness, a silence will envelop you. The meditation is so powerful that you will spontaneously
become an observer to the body and the the mind.
In fact this is the focal point of the meditation: the
previous stages are a preparation to the silence –
meditation.

In the fifth stage, dance, sing, rejoice in celebration and thanksgiving.

If you cannot make noise in the place where you
are meditating, an alternative method is given. In
this, all the sounds are kept within, rather than
being thrown out. For those who enter it fully, the
meditation can go very deep. In the second stage
allow the body to explode into a soundless
catharsis through body movements. In the third
stage hammer the sound "hoo" deep inside. Fifth
stage: dance.

When the sleep is broken, the whole nature
becomes alive; the night has gone, the darkness is no more, the sun is coming up, and
everything becomes conscious and alert. This
is a meditation in which you have to be continuously alert, conscious, aware, whatsoever
you do. Remain a witness. Don't get lost.

Once it happened – two dogs were
watching people do the Dynamic meditation,
and I heard one dog say to the other: When I
do this my master gives me worm pills.

Third stage: ten minutes (above)

With raised arms, jump up and down shouting the mantra "hoo, hoo, hoo!" as deeply as possible. Each time you land, on the flats of your feet, let the sound hammer deep into your sexual center (about one or two landings per second). You may get a stitch in your belly, slow down slightly and breathe into the pain and rather than shouting the mantra, breathe it out, don't stop. Give all you have, exhaust yourself totally.

Fourth stage: fifteen minutes

Stop! Freeze where you are in whatever position you find yourself. Don't arrange the body in any way. A cough, a movement, anything will dissipate the energy flow and the effort will be lost. Be a witness to everything that is happening.

Fifth stage: fifteen minutes

Celebrate and rejoice with music and dance, expressing your gratitude towards everything around you. Carry your happiness with you throughout the day.

Kundalini

Meditation has its own movement; you can't direct it,
shape it or force it, if you do, it ceases to be meditation.

J. Krishnamurti

The Kundalini meditation in its present form was created by Bhagwan Shree Rajneesh as a technique for moving very potent energies through the body. It can be done in late afternoon or around sunset on an empty stomach. Its purpose is to shake off the tensions of the whole day and to start the evening afresh.

When you are doing the Kundalini meditation, then allow the shaking, don't do it. Stand silently, feel it coming and when your body starts a little trembling, help it but don't do it. Enjoy it, feel blissful about it, allow it, receive it, welcome it, but don't will it.

If you force it it will become an exercise, a bodily physical exercise. Then the shaking will be there but just on the surface, it will not penetrate you. You will remain solid, stone-like, rock-like within; you will remain the ma-

nipulator, the doer, and the body will just be following. The body is not the question – you are the question.

When I say shake I mean your solidity, your rock-like being should shake to the very foundations so that it becomes liquid, fluid, melts, flows. And when the rock-like being becomes liquid, your body will follow. Then there is no shake, only shaking. Then nobody is doing it, it is simply happening. Then the doer is not.

The Dynamic meditation, or the Kundalini, or the Nadabrahma, these are not really meditations. You are just getting in tune. It is like... if you have seen Indian classical musicians playing. For half an hour, or sometimes even more, they simply go on fixing their instruments. They will move their knobs, they will make the strings tight or

First stage: 15 minutes (above left)
Be loose and let your whole body shake, feeling the
energies moving up from your feet. Let go
everywhere and become the shaking. Your eyes may
be open or closed.

Second stage: 15 minutes (above right)
Dance... any way you feel, and let the whole body
move as it wishes.

loose, and the drum player will go on checking
his drum – whether it is perfect or not. For
half an hour they go on doing this. This is not
music, this is just preparation.

Kundalini is not really meditation. It is just
preparation. You are preparing your instrument. When it is ready, then you stand in
silence, then meditation starts. Then you are
utterly there. You have woken yourself up by
jumping, by dancing, by breathing, by
shouting – these are all devices to make you a
little more alert than you ordinarily are. Once
you are alert, then the waiting begins.

Waiting is meditation. Waiting with full
awareness. And then it comes, it descends on
you, it surrounds you, it plays around you, it
dances around you, it cleanses you, it purifies
you, it transforms you.

Third stage: 15 minutes (left)
Close your eyes and be still, sitting or standing...
witnessing whatever is happening inside and out.

Fourth stage: 15 minutes (below)
Keeping your eyes closed, lie down and be still.

Gourishankar

I honor those who try to rid themselves of any lying,
who empty the self and have only clear being there.

Rumi

This technique consists of four stages of 15 minutes each and can be done anytime. The first two stages prepare the meditator for the spontaneous Latihan of the third stage. In the Latihan you just stand and let your body move, very slowly and gently, a bit like in Tai Chi. You allow any movement that wants to come to happen, you are not doing the movement. The Latihan is the receiving of God – put simply, to receive the Latihan is just to wait and let things happen – no pushing, no determination or willful effort. If the breathing is done correctly in the first stage the carbon dioxide formed in the blood stream will make you feel as high as Gourishankar (Mt. Everest).

The first three stages should be accompanied by a steady rhythmic beat, preferably combined with a soothing background music. The beat should be seven times the normal heartbeat and, if possible, the flashing light should be a synchronized strobe.

First stage: 15 minutes
Sit with closed eyes. Inhale deeply through the nose, filling the lungs. Hold the breath for as long as possible, then exhale gently through the mouth and keep the lungs empty for as long as possible. Continue this breathing cycle throughout the first stage.

Second stage: 15 minutes (far left)
Return to normal breathing and with a gentle gaze look at a candle flame or a flashing blue light. Keep your body still.

Third stage: 15 minutes (left)
With closed eyes, stand up and let your body be loose and receptive. The subtle energies will be felt to move the body outside your normal control. Allow this Latihan to happen. Do not do the moving: let moving happen, gently and gracefully.

Fourth stage: 15 minutes (below)
Lie down with closed eyes, silent and still.

Nadabrahma

Nadabrahma is an ancient Tibetan Buddhist technique which was originally done in the early hours of the morning. It is suggested that it should be done either at night before going to sleep or during the morning, then it should be followed by at least 15 minutes rest. It can be done alone, with others or even at work. It is good done on an empty stomach, otherwise the inner sound cannot go very deep. (Also see section on humming in previous chapter)

Nadabrahma for couples

Partners sit facing each other, covered by a bed sheet and holding each other's crossed hands. It is best to wear no other clothing. Light the room only by four small candles and burn a particular incense, kept only for this meditation.

Close your eyes and hum together for thirty minutes. After a short while the energies will be felt to meet, merge and unite.

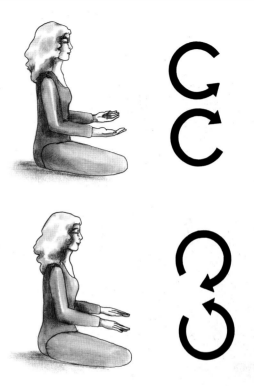

Some things are to understand but not say. Be quiet.

Rumi

First stage: 30 minutes
Sit in a relaxed position with eyes closed and lips together. Start humming, loudly enough to be heard by others and create a vibration throughout your body. You can visualize a hollow tube or an empty vessel, filled only with the vibrations of the humming. A point will come when the humming continues by itself and you become the listener. There is no special breathing and you can alter the pitch or move your body smoothly and slowly if you feel like it. The body is activated and every fiber cleansed. (It is particularly useful in healing.)

Second stage: 15 minutes
The second stage is divided into two sections. For the first half (above top), move the hands, palms up, in an outward circular motion. Starting at the navel, both hands move forwards and then divide to make two large circles mirroring each other left and right. The movement should be so slow that at times there will appear to be no movement at all. Feel that you are giving energy outwards to the universe.
After seven and a half minutes turn the hands, palm down, and start moving them in the opposite direction (above bottom). Now the hands will come together towards the navel and divide outwards to the sides of the body. Feel that you are taking energy in. As in the first stage, don't inhibit any soft, slow movements of the rest of your body.

Third stage: 15 minutes
Sit or lie absolutely quiet and still.

Vipassana

*Meditation is not a search;
it's not a seeking,
a probing, an exploration.
It is an explosion and discovery.*

J. Krishnamurti

Twenty-five centuries ago Gautam Buddha gave this method of inner witnessing to his thousands of disciples, many of whom became enlightened. Vipassana is simply a way of witnessing.

It is an invitation to watch yourself – your mind, your emotions, your body, your environment – without reacting to what you observe. It is an invitation to get to know yourself honestly and sincerely, to make friends with yourself, and to realize that the witnessing self is not identified with what is being seeing. Success and failure are not part of meditation, and nothing special is supposed to happen. There is nothing to expect.

Mind is tricky, and is not used to being observed at work and play. Excuses not to meditate, not to sit, not to have time, not to be comfortable will arise at first. It helps to meditate at a regular, pre-selected time and place. But anytime is better than no-time, and anywhere is better than nowhere.

Sitting with a friend makes things easier. Remember that silence does not mean you can't enjoy, and having a group of friends meditate together is a beautiful experience.

Vipassana is the meditation that has made more people in the world enlightened than

any other, because it is the very essence. All other meditations have the same essence, but in different forms; something non-essential is also joined with them. But Vipassana is pure essence. You cannot drop anything out of it and you cannot add anything to improve it.

Vipassana is such a simple thing that even a small child can do it. In fact, the smallest child can do it better than you, because he is not yet filled with the garbage of the mind; he is still clean and innocent. Vipassana can be done in three ways – you can choose which one suits you best.

The first is: awareness of your actions, your body, your mind, your heart. Walking, you should walk with awareness. Moving your hand, you should move with awareness, knowing perfectly that you are moving the hand. You can move it without any consciousness, like a mechanical thing... you are on a morning walk; you can go on walking without being aware of your feet.

Be alert of the movements of your body. While eating, be alert to the movements that are needed for eating. Taking a shower, be alert to the coolness that is coming to you, the water falling on you and the tremendous joy of it – just be alert. Any of these activities should not go on happening in an unconscious state.

And the same about your mind. Whatever thought passes on the screen of your mind, just be a watcher. Whatever emotion passes on the screen of your heart, just remain a witness – don't get involved, don't get identified, don't evaluate what is good, what is bad; that is not part of your meditation.

The second form is breathing, becoming aware of breathing. As the breath goes in, your belly starts rising up, and as the breath

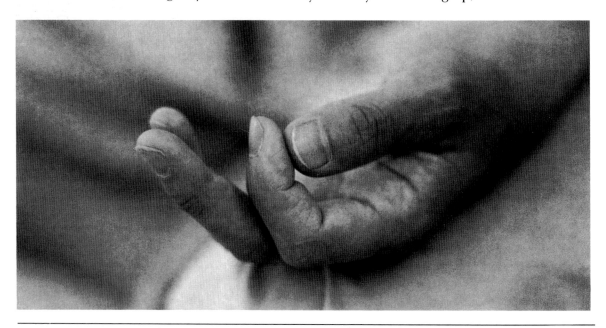

goes out, your belly starts settling down again. So the second method is to be aware of the belly: its rising and falling. Just the very awareness of the belly rising and falling... and the belly is very close to the life sources because the child is joined with the mother's life through the navel. Behind the navel is his life's source. So, when the belly rises up, it is really the life energy, the spring of life that is rising up and falling down with each breath. That too is not difficult, and perhaps maybe even easier because it is a single technique.

In the first, you have to be aware of the body, you have to be aware of the mind, you have to be aware of your emotions, moods. So it has three steps. The second approach is a single step: just the belly, moving up and down. And the result is the same. As you become more aware of the belly, the mind becomes silent, the heart becomes silent, the moods disappear.

And the third is to be aware of the breath at the entrance when the breath goes in through your nostrils. Feel it at that extreme – the other polarity from the belly – feel it from the nose. The breath going in gives a certain coolness to your nostrils. Then the breath going out... breath going in, breath going out.

That too is possible. It is easier for men than for women. The woman is more aware of the belly. Most of the men don't even breathe as deep as the belly. Their chest rises up and falls down, because a wrong kind of athletics prevails over the world. Certainly it gives a more beautiful form to the body if your chest is high and your belly is almost non-existent. Man has chosen to breathe only up to the

chest, so the chest becomes bigger and bigger and the belly shrinks down. That appears to him to be more athletic.

Around the world, except in Japan, all athletes and teachers of athletes emphasize to breathe by filling your lungs, expanding your chest, and pulling the belly in. The ideal is the lion whose chest is big and whose belly is very small. So be like a lion; that has become the rule for athletic gymnasts, and the people who have been working with the body.

Japan is the only exception where they don't care that the chest should be broad and the belly should be pulled in. It needs a certain discipline to pull the belly in; it is not natural. Japan has chosen the natural way, hence you

the whole night you were breathing naturally... you were in Japan!

These are the two points: if you are afraid that breathing from the belly and being attentive to its rising and falling will destroy your athletic form... men may be more interested in that athletic form. Then for them it is easier to watch near the nostrils where the breath enters. Watch, and when the breath goes out, watch.

These are the three forms. Any one will do. And if you want to do two forms together, you can do two forms together; then the effort will become more intense. If you want to do all the three forms together, you can do all three forms together. Then the possibilities will be quicker. But it all depends on you, whatever feels easy. Remember: easy is right.

As meditation becomes settled and mind silent, the ego will disappear. You will be there, but there will be no feeling of "I". Then the doors are open.

Just wait with a loving longing, with a welcome in the heart for that great moment – the greatest moment in anybody's life – of enlightenment.

It comes... it certainly comes. It has never delayed for a single moment. Once you are in the right tuning, it suddenly explodes in you, transforms you. The old man is dead and the new man has arrived.

Sitting meditation

Find a place where you can sit comfortably, undisturbed, without sleeping for 40-60 minutes. Although this is the ideal time you can also sit for just 20 minutes – anywhere, anytime. Your back and head should be straight. If needed it is fine to

will be surprises to see a Japanese statue of Buddha. That is the way you can immediately discriminate whether the statue is Indian or Japanese. The Indian statues of Gautam Buddha have a very athletic body; the belly is very small and the chest is very broad. But the Japanese Buddha is totally different; his chest is almost silent, because he breathes from the belly, but his belly is bigger. It doesn't look very good – because the idea prevalent in the world is so old, but breathing from the belly is more natural, more relaxed.

In the night it happens when you sleep; you don't breathe from the chest, you breathe from the belly. That's why the night is such a relaxed experience. After your sleep, in the morning you feel so fresh, so young, because

use a chair. Your eyes are best closed, and your breathing should be as it usually is; easy is right. Stay as still as you can, moving only if it is really necessary. If you move, notice how and why you are moving.

While sitting the primary object of attention is the rise and fall of your belly – just above the navel – caused by breathing in and out. It is not a concentration technique, so when other things come into the field of your awareness, while watching your breath, these too are part of your meditation. Nothing is a distraction in Vipassana. When something takes your attention go with it. Place your whole attention on it, whatever it is. When your attention is free, then go back to your breathing.

It is the process of watching which is the meditation, not what you are watching. Remember not to become identified with, or lost in whatever comes up: thoughts, feelings, judg-

ments, body sensations, impressions from outside, and the whole world which constantly snatches your attention from yourself.

If questions or problems arise which require an answer, let them remain a mystery until your meditation time is over.

Walking meditation

In this technique you bring your whole attention to your feet as they touch the ground. Walk slowly, ordinarily, with your awareness focused on your feet as they touch the earth.

Walk in a circle or a straight line, indoors or outdoors, it doesn't matter. Do whatever you enjoy most. Keep your eyes lowered so that you can only see the ground a few steps ahead. If other things take your attention, notice them, give them all your awareness. When they have lost their attraction return your attention to your feet.

As in sitting, witnessing is the process, but the primary objects are the feet as they walk, not the belly as it breathes. The period for walking should be 20-30 minutes or it can be combined with 45 minutes of sitting followed by 15 minutes of walking.

General awareness meditation

Anything can become your primary object for witnessing. Slowing down, doing one thing at a time you can become aware of what you are doing, while you are doing it. This can include not only actions but intentions too. Everything in your daily routine: eating, washing up, cleaning the house, smoking, telephoning, chatting over a cup a tea, dancing, flirting, reading, everything can become a meditation; all you need is awareness. Meditation can be fun and can enrich the quality of ordinary life.

Zazen

When you simply are,
you are in alignment
with the isness of all things;
and through that alignment,
you may have anything you desire –
and you have to do nothing except be!

Ramtha

Zazen is deep unoccupiedness, it is not even meditation, because when you meditate you are trying to do something: remembering being God or even remembering yourself. These efforts create ripples.

You can sit anywhere, but whatsoever you are looking at should not be too exciting. For example things should not be moving too much. They become a distraction. You can watch the trees – that is not a problem because they are not moving and the scene remains constant. You can watch the sky or just sit in the corner watching the wall.

The second thing is, don't look at anything in particular – just emptiness, because the eyes are there and one has to look at something, but you are not looking at anything in

An ancient pond
A frog jumps in
Plop!

Basho

particular. Don't focus or concentrate on anything – just a diffuse image. That relaxes very much. And the third thing, relax your breathing. Don't do it, let it happen. Let it be natural and that will relax even more.

The fourth thing is, let your body remain as immobile as possible. First find a good posture – you can sit on a pillow or mattress or whatsoever you feel, but once you settle, remain immobile, because if the body does not move, the mind automatically falls silent. In a moving body, the mind also continues to move, because body-mind are not two things. They are one... it is one energy.

In the beginning it will seem a little difficult but after a few days you will enjoy it tremendously. You will see, by and by, layer upon layer of the mind starting to drop. A moment comes when you are simply there with no mind.

Bodhidharma sat for nine years just facing the wall, doing nothing – just sitting for nine years. The tradition has it that his legs withered away. To me that is symbolic. It simply means that all movements withered away because all motivation withered away. He was not going anywhere. There was no desire to move, no goal to achieve – and he achieved the greatest that is possible. He is one of the rarest souls that have ever walked on earth. And just sitting before a wall he achieved everything; not doing anything, no technique, no method, nothing. This was the only technique. When there is nothing to see, by and by your interest in seeing disappears. By just facing a plain wall, inside you a parallel emptiness and plainness arises. Parallel to the wall another wall arises – of no-thought.

Fundamentally no wisdom-tree exists,
Nor the stand of a mirror bright.
Since all is Void from the beginning
Where can the dust alight?

Hui Neng

Nataraj

Meditation is a function of being happy.
Meditation follows a happy man like a shadow.
Wherever he goes, whatsoever he is doing, he is meditative.

OSHO

Forget the dancer, the center of the ego; become the dance. That is the meditation. Dance so deeply that you forget completely that *you* are dancing and begin to feel that you are the dance. The division must disappear; then it becomes a meditation. If the division is there, then it is an exercise: good, healthy, but it cannot be said to be spiritual. It is just a simple dance. Dance is good in itself – as far as it goes, it is good. After it, you will feel fresh, young. But it is not meditation yet. The dancer must go, until only the dance remains.

So what to do? Be totally in the dance, because division can exist only if you are not total in it. If you are standing aside and looking at your own dance, the division will remain: you are the dancer and you are dancing. Then dancing is just an act, something you are doing; it is not your being. So get involved totally; be merged in it. Don't stand aside, don't be an observer. Participate!

Let the dance flow in its own way; don't force it. Rather, follow it; allow it to happen. It is not a doing but a happening. Remain in the mood of festivity. You are not doing something very serious; you're just playing, playing with your life energy, playing with your bio-energy, allowing it to move in its own way. Just like the wind blows and the river flows – you are flowing and blowing. Feel it.

And be playful. Remember this word "playful" always – with me, it is very basic. In this country we call creation God's *leela* – God's play. God has not created the world; it is his play.

First stage: 40 minutes
With eyes open or closed dance as if possessed. Let your unconscious take over completely. Do not control your movements or be a witness to what is happening. Just be totally in the dance.

Second stage: 20 minutes
Lie down immediately. Be silent and still. Allow the vibrations of the dance and the music to penetrate your most subtle layers.

Third stage: 5 minutes
Dance in celebration and enjoy.

Prayer

I saw you last night in the gathering,
but could not take you openly in my arms,
so I put my lips next to your cheek,
pretending to talk privately.

Rumi

It is best to do this prayer at night, in a darkened room, going to sleep immediately afterwards; or it can be done in the morning, but it must be followed by fifteen minutes rest. This rest is necessary, otherwise you will feel as if you are drunk, in a stupor. This merging with energy is prayer. It changes you. And when *you* change, the whole existence changes. Raise both your hands towards the sky, palms uppermost, head up, just feeling existence flowing in you.

As the energy flows down your arms you will feel a gentle tremor – be like a leaf in a breeze, trembling. Allow it, help it. Then let your whole body vibrate with energy, and just let whatever happens happen.

You feel again a flowing with the earth. Earth and heaven, above and below, yin and yang, male and female – you float, you mix, you drop yourself completely. You are not. You become one... merge.

After two to three minutes, or whenever you feel completely filled, lean down to the earth and kiss the earth. You simply become a vehicle to allow the divine energy to unite with that of the earth.

These two stages should be repeated six more times so that each of the *chakras* (see Chakra breathing meditation) can become unblocked. You can repeat it more than six times, but if you do less than six times you will feel restless and unable to sleep.

Go into sleep in that very state of prayer. Just fall asleep and the energy will be there. You will be flowing with it, falling into sleep. That will help very greatly because then the energy will surround you the whole night and it will continue to work. By the morning you will feel fresher than you have ever felt before, more vital than you have ever felt before. A new plan, a new life will start penetrating you, and the whole day you will feel full of new energy; a new vibe, a new song in your heart, and a new dance in your step.

No-mind

I cannot open the doors of heaven first
and you cannot become silent. Be totally mad first.

OSHO

This meditation can be done alone but it is better to do it together with a group of friends. Find a room where you can make a lot of noise and where you will not be disturbed.

Try the meditation for seven days at first. That will be a good time period to experience the effects of the meditation. Then after that you can continue it or repeat it as you feel to. It is generally suggested that the Gibberish be done for 45 minutes to an hour, followed by a period of silent Witnessing for 45 minutes to and hour – but this timing is not mandatory. The Let-Go is to be done just a few minutes at the end of the meditation.

Have someone to time it and use a drum to indicate the beginning of each stage.

The first part is Gibberish. The word "Gibberish" comes from a Sufi mystic Jabbar. Jabbar never spoke any language, he just uttered nonsense. Still, he had thousands of disciples because what he was saying was: "Your mind is nothing but gibberish. Put it aside and you will have a taste of your own being." To use Gibberish, don't say things which are meaningful, don't use the language that you know. Use Chinese if you don't know Chinese. Use Japanese if you don't know Japanese. Use German if you don't know German. For the first time have freedom... the same as all the birds have. Simply allow whatever comes to your mind without bothering about its rationality, reasonability, meaning, significance, just the way the birds are doing. For the first part, leave language and mind aside.

Allow yourself to express whatever needs to be expressed within you. Throw everything out. The mind thinks, always, in terms of words. Gibberish helps to break up this pattern of continual verbalization. Without suppressing your thoughts, you can throw them out – in Gibberish. Let your body likewise be expressive.

Awareness is always present – surrounded by your Gibberish, which has to be taken out. That is your poison. So first throw out all your rubbish, gibberish, insanity. Then the silence descends. Have a taste of this tremendous silence. This is what I have called the quantum leap from mind to no-mind.

Everything is allowed: sing, cry, shout, mumble, talk, whisper. But do not let empty spaces happen. If you cannot find sounds to gibber with, just say lalalalala, but do not remain there doing nothing. Likewise you can let your body do what it wants: jump, lay down, sit, kick and so on.

If you do this meditation with other people do not relate or interfere with them in any way. Just stay with what is happening to you and don't bother about what the others are doing; they are all throwing their garbage, if you listen you may catch it, so it is better to mind your own business.

Out of this will arise the second part, a great silence in which you have to close your eyes and freeze your body, all its movements, gather your energies within yourself. Remain here and now.

In the third part... relax your body and let it fall without any effort, without your mind controlling. Just fall like a bag of rice. Each segment will begin with the sound of a drum.

The mystic rose

Your heart is the soil,
your trust is the climate
and your being is the mystic rose –
its opening, blossoming, releasing its fragrance.

OSHO

The mystic rose is just a symbol of the man whose being is dormant no more, is asleep no more, but is fully awake and has opened all its petals and has become sensitive to all that is truthful, beautiful, good – the very splendor of existence.

This unique meditation brings out the freshness and the wonder of the child within you. It is an absolutely new meditation which never existed before in the history of mankind. It will be a deep cleansing of many wounds and the scars of centuries. Society has repressed laughter and crying because they disturb the status quo; this has been going on for millennia. We have been so much repressed and whatever is repressed in this way becomes a wound. These wounds and scars have been developing for many lives. They are not part

of the body – they are surrounding the consciousness and process that is available to us.

The Mystic Rose meditation is the first major breakthrough since Vipassana 25 centuries ago. Vipassana worked for Gautam the Buddha because he had spent 29 years in a palace enjoying everything... laughing, weeping, dancing, loving. So he had no repres-sions. But nobody else is in Gautam the Buddha's situation, yet for 25 centuries thousands of Buddhists have been doing Vipassana and they have simply become dry and desert-like. Even smiling is difficult for them. The problem is that witnessing alone is automatically suppressing... weeping stops when you witness it, but becomes dormant. When a man reaches into his innermost being he will find that the first layer is of laughter and the second layer is of agony, tears. This new meditation technique gets rid of the laughing and weeping beforehand so there is nothing left to suppress in the witnessing and the witnessing simply opens a pure sky.

Every society has done so much harm by preventing your joys and your tears. Your laughter has been repressed; you have been told, "Don't laugh, it is a serious matter." You are not allowed to laugh in a church, or in a university class. If you just stand on the street and start crying and a crowd will gather to console you: "Don't cry! Whatever has happened forget all about it, it has happened." Nobody knows what has happened, nobody can help you, but everybody will try – "Don't cry!" And the reason is that if you go on crying, then *they* will start crying, because they are also flooded with tears. Those tears are very close to the eyes.

This meditation is going to become worldwide, without any doubt, because its effects will show anybody that the person has become younger, the person has become more loving, the person has become graceful. The person has become more joyful, more a celebrant.

And it is healthy to cry, to weep, to laugh. Now scientists are discovering that crying, weeping, laughter, are immensely healthful, not only physically but also psychologically. They are very much capable of keeping you sane. The whole of humanity has gone a little cuckoo for the simple reason that nobody laughs fully.

The meditation is best done in a group but can also be done alone. Find a space where you will not

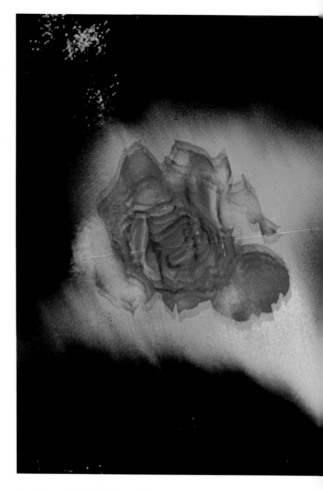

be disturbed. It lasts for 21 days. The first part, laughter, lasts for seven days, three hours a day. The second part, tears, also lasts for seven days, three hours a day. The third part, the watcher on the hills, is the same – three hours a day for seven days. If three hours is not possible in your circumstances, then follow your feelings as to the timing that suits you.

The first part begins with saying "yaa-hoo!" raising both arms in the air. There is no meaning in

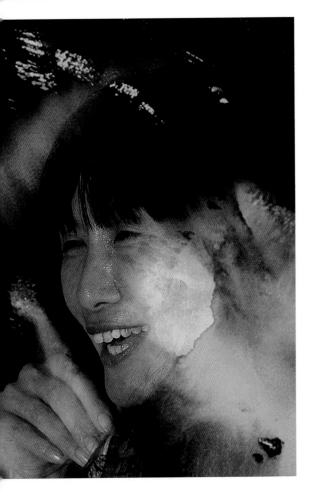

the words "yaa-hoo" and "yaa-boo". These are simply techniques, sounds which can be used for a certain purpose, to enter into your own being. For example "om" has no meaning, it is not part of any alphabet, but it has some existential purpose: it provokes in you the sound of the eternal. It is something similar to the sound of existence itself – not exactly the same, a faraway echo, but still very representative. The words "yaa-hoo" and "yaa-boo" work in the same way.

So begin with "yaa-hoo!" and then laugh for three hours. Simply laugh for no reason at all. And whenever your laughter starts dying, again say, "yaa-hoo!" and it will come back. Find your own inner source of laughter, your original spontaneous laugh. It is there, so don't worry, it will come. Then end with "yaa-hoo!"

In the second part begin with "yaa-boo!" and then cry for three hours. Just cry for no reason. At the end of the three hours, end with "yaa-boo".

We go into laughter first because it is easier; crying has been repressed more deeply than laughing. There will be no talking in the group. It is important during the laughter not to cry, and not to laugh during the tears. Just start laughing. If someone in the group is not laughing, the other members of the group can lovingly tickle him or her. And if someone cannot cry, then the other members can just softly touch him and share their tears with him. If it is difficult for the person to laugh or cry, they should talk gibberish – as if mad – until the laughter or the tears be released: you will feel like a new man.

Three hours has been chosen because one hour is not enough. When the laughing and crying break, it is just like a dam breaking. The question is how to break the dam. You will find it very refreshing.

In the third part, the watcher on the hills, you just sit, comfortably and alert, for 45 minutes watching your breath coming in and going out (see Vipassana). Then dance for 15 minutes with heartful music – and keep watching during the dance. Then sit again for 45 minutes, dance again for 15 minutes, sit for 45 minutes and finish with 15 minutes dancing.

Whirling

*You do not see that the Real is in your home,
and you wander from forest to forest listlessly!*

Kabir

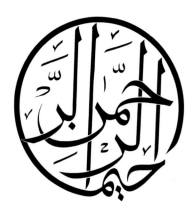

The ancient Indian Sufis, a religious group, practiced the Whirling meditation – perhaps one of the most beautiful and exciting meditations of all. Be prepared, this one will knock your head off! Sufi Whirling is one of the most ancient techniques, one of the most forceful. It is so deep that even a single experience can make you totally different. Whirl with open eyes, just like small children go on twirling, as if your inner being has become a center and your whole body has become a wheel, moving, a potter's wheel, moving. You are in the center, but the whole body is moving.

It is recommended that no food or drink be taken for three hours before whirling. It is best to have bare feet and wear loose clothing. The meditation is divided into two stages, whirling and resting. There is no fixed time for the whirling – it can go on for hours – but it is suggested that you continue for at least an hour to get fully into the feeling of the energy whirlpool.

For those who have never gone into such physical movement – a few simple pointers:

Start with your hands crossed onto your shoulders and remember that you can always return your hands to this position if you ever feel dizzy. Rotate on your left foot in short twists, using your right foot to drive your body around the left foot. Your left foot is like an anchor to the ground so that if you lose your balance, think of your left foot, direct your attention towards it and this will help to bring your balance back.

The whirling is done on the spot in an anti-

(Above)
The right hand held high, palm upwards and the left hand held shoulder height, palm downwards, turn in an anti-clockwise motion using your left foot as an anchor.

(Above)
Put your left hand on your right shoulder, then put your right hand on your left shoulder. Use this position to start and end the meditation. You can also use it to recover your balance or if you experience pain in your arms during the whirling.

(Above)
If you feel nauseous, drop your head between your legs, with your arms folded on your chest. Keep this position until the ill feeling disappears.

clockwise direction, with the right arm held high, palm upwards, and the left arm held low, palm downwards. People who feel discomfort from whirling anti-clockwise can change to clockwise. Let your body be soft and keep your eyes open, but unfocused so that images become blurred and flowing. For the first 15 minutes, rotate slowly. Then gradually build up speed over the next 30 minutes, the whirling takes over and you become a whirlpool of energy – the periphery a storm of movement but the witness at the center still.

When you are whirling so fast that you cannot remain upright, your body will fall by itself. Don't make the fall a decision on your part nor attempt to arrange the landing in advance; if your body is soft you will land softly and the earth will absorb your energy.

If the idea of letting yourself fall is too much then allow yourself to slow down very slowly. If you have been whirling for an hour then the process of slowing down might take some time – even ten minutes or more.

Once you have fallen, the second part of the meditation starts. Roll onto your stomach immediately so that your bare navel is in contact with the earth. If anybody feels strong discomfort lying this way, he should lie on his back. Feel your body blending into the earth, like a small child pressed to his mother's breasts. Keep your eyes closed and remain passive and silent for at least 15 minutes.

After the meditation be as quiet and inactive as possible.

Some people may feel nauseous during the whirling meditation, but this feeling should disappear within two or three days. Only discontinue the meditation if it persists. As an immediate cure for nausea simply drop your head between your legs – an old remedy!

SYMBOL	COLOR	SANSKRIT	POSITION	FUNCTION
	Red	Muladhara	Center of the lower pelvis, and between the base of the spine in the back and the pubic area in the front	Sexuality, grounding, physical coordination and survival
	Orange	Svadhisthana	Four fingers below the navel	Sensuality, the ability to feel emotions and contentment
	Yellow	Manipura	Solar plexus area, above the navel and below the breast bone	Gives vitality, power, the strength to express emotions and to have the integrity to be oneself
	Green	Anahata	Middle of the chest in the area of the breast bone	Unconditional love and peace; it gives the ability to love oneself and others unconditionally
	Blue	Visuddha	Throat area	Creativity, receptivity and the ability to communicate
	Indigo	Ajna	Called the third eye, it lies in the middle of the head, behind the point between the eyebrows	Inner vision, intuition and the ability to know oneself
	Violet	Sahasrara	Inside the top of the head and extends above the head	Opening to the universal consciousness

GLAND	AREA GOVERNED
Gonads	Reproductive organs
Adrenals	Spinal column, kidneys
Pancreas	Stomach, liver, gall bladder, nervous system
Thymus	Heart, blood, vagus nerve, circulatory system
Thyroid	Bronchial and vocal apparatus, lungs, alimentary canal
Pituitary	Lower brain, left eye, ears, nose, nervous system
Pineal	Upper brain, right eye

Chakra breathing

Man has to pass through all the seven chakras, seven chakras towards the divine.
OSHO

Man is a rainbow because a rainbow will give you the total perspective in which man can be understood – from the lowest to the highest. The rainbow has seven colors; man has seven centers of his being. The allegory of seven is very ancient. In India, the allegory has taken the form of seven chakras: the lowest is *muladhara* and the highest is *sahasrara*, and between these two are five steps, five more chakras. Man has to pass through all these seven chakras – seven steps towards the divine.

Chakra breathing meditation can help you to become aware of and experience each of the seven chakras. This meditation is active and uses deep rapid breathing and body movement to open and bring awareness and vitality to the chakras. The meditation enables you to bring silence and vitality into your everyday life.

The location of the chakras in the body indicated in the chart are just guidelines. You can discover for yourself the exact location of each chakra in your own body. Also, the chakras tend to be located towards the center of the body from front to back, and connect into the spine; in other words, they are three-dimensional.

This meditation is best done on an empty stomach in the early morning or late afternoon before dinner.

In the first stage of this meditation, start by standing with feet as wide apart as your hips or shoulders. Let your body be loose and relaxed. Close your eyes and with your mouth open breathe deeply and rapidly (about an in and an out in one second) into the first chakra. As you breathe let your attention be in the pelvic area of your body, where the first chakra is located. Equal emphasis should be put on both the in and out breaths. Don't force your breathing: breathe in a rhythm that feels comfortable and allows you to become aware of the feelings and sensations of each chakra. Breathe into the first chakra for about a minute and a half and then move into the second chakra.

Go on moving this deep rapid breathing up into the next chakra – the third, then the fourth, fifth, sixth and the seventh chakra. As you breathe up from chakra to chakra your breathing should become more rapid and more gentle, so that you are taking about twice as many breaths (in, out, in, out in one second) in the seventh chakra as you were in the first.

While breathing, it is helpful to shake your body, stretch, tilt or rotate your pelvis and move your hands in any way that you feel but let your feet stay in one spot. Allow your feet, knees, hips, and other joints to become like springs so that once you set the breathing and body into motion, the movement will become continuous and effortless.

Let your awareness remain primarily with the sensation of the chakras, rather than with the breathing or the body movement.

After breathing in the seventh chakra for a while, let your breath and awareness turn and fall back down through each chakra. As you breathe down allow your breath to become slower from chakra to chakra. Let the energy flow down by itself from the seventh chakra to include the entire spectrum of chakra energy from top to bottom, like seven colors blending into one rainbow. This downward breathing should take about two minutes and it is up to you how long you breathe into each chakra.

After you finish this sequence, stand silently for a few moments before starting the next sequence. This upward and downward breathing sequence should be repeated three times, or for a total of about 45 minutes. If you don't feel the energy of your chakras at first, just breathe into the area where they are located. Remember not too push the breath – instead, allow the breath and body movement to be like a bridge and carry you into the sensations and qualities of energy of each chakra. Becoming sensitive to the different qualities of each chakra comes not through force, but through awareness and patience.

In the second stage, after the third breathing sequence, sit with closed eyes in silence for at least 15 minutes, or longer if you wish. As you sit don't focus on anything in particular. Allow yourself to become aware of and watch whatever is happening within.

Above all, do this meditation only if it feels good and if it takes you deeper into peace, joy and bliss. If it starts bringing up emotions that are disturbing, it is recommended that you try a cathartic meditation instead, such as Dynamic meditation.

EPILOGUE

The sequence of drawings on the following pages are of Taoist origin. Their purpose is to represent the inexpressible, using the Ox as the metaphor for the spiritual search of the disciple. Nobody knows how the paintings came into existence, but in the twelfth Century, Kakuan, a Chinese Zen Master, updated and repainted them in the form depicted here. The Taoist paintings finished with the eighth: the void, the emptiness, but Kakuan added two other configurations. He affirmed that this was not the end: one returns to the world, and only then the circle will be complete. Naturally one returns to the market place completely changed, but not alone, one returns with a bottle of wine: drunk with the divine, to help others to become drunk as well. This is the spirit of meditation.

distant mountains (when one has nothing to identify with, at first one feels lost), my strength failing and my vitality exhausted, I cannot find the bull. I only hear the locusts chirring through the forest at night.

The bull (symbol of energy, vitality and dynamism, life itself in its full sense – indicating the inner force, the inner potential) never has been lost. What need is there to search? Only because of separation from my true nature I fail to find him (you *are* this energy but you are not aware of what this energy is). In the confusion of the senses I lose even its tracks (a moment comes when one is exhausted from the search and moves in confusion, that is the moment when the search really starts). Far from home, I see many crossroads, but which way is the right one I know not. Greed and fear, good and bad, entangle me.

The search for the bull
In the pastures of this world, I endlessly push aside the tall grasses (the desires) in search of the bull. Following unnamed rivers, lost upon the interpenetrating paths of

Discovering the footprints
Along the riverbank under the trees, I discover footprints! Even under the fragrant grass I see his prints. Deep in remote mountains they are found. These traces no more can be hidden than one's nose looking heavenward.

Understanding the teachings (not an intellectual understanding, but an existential understanding), I see the footprints of the bull. Then I learn that just as many utensils are made from one metal, so too are myriad entities made of the fabric of self. Unless I discriminate how will I perceive the true from the untrue? Not yet having entered the gate, nevertheless I have discerned the path.

Catching the bull

I seize him with a terrific struggle. His great will and power are inexhaustible. He charges to the high plateau far above the cloud-mists, or in an impenetrable ravine he stands.

He dwelt in the forest a long time, but I caught him today. Infatuation for scenery interferes with his direction. Longing for sweeter grass, he wanders away. His mind still is stubborn and unbridled. If I wish him to submit, I must raise my whip.

Taming the bull

The whip (awareness) and rope (inner discipline) are necessary. Else he might stray off down some dusty road. Being well trained he becomes naturally gentle. Then, unfettered, he obeys his master.

When one thought arises, another thought follows. When the first thought springs from Enlightenment, all subsequent thoughts are true. Through delusion, one makes everything untrue. Delusion is not caused by objectivity; it is the result of subjectivity (The world is not causing the illusion, you are causing it, it is created by your mind). Hold the nose-ring and do no allow even a doubt.

Perceiving the bull

I hear the song of the nightingale. The sun is warm, the wind is mild, willows are green along the shore. Here no bull can hide! Which artist can draw that massive head, those majestic horns?

When one hears the voice, one can sense its source. As soon as the six senses merge, the gate is entered (when you become sensitive to whatever happens to you and around you it is meditation, being available to whatever happens around, without choice). Wherever one enters one sees the head of the bull! This unity is like salt in water, like color in dyestuff. The slightest thing is not apart from self.

Riding the bull home

Mounting the bull, slowly I return homeward (when you are not the master, you will move away from home). The voice of my flute intones through the evening (your bliss and celebration is the sign of whether or not you are on the path. If you are blissful, then you can tell that you are on the right track). Measuring with hand-beats the pulsating harmony, I direct the endless rhythm. Whoever hears this melody will join me.

This struggle is over; gain and loss are assimilated. I sing the song of the village woodsman, and I play the tunes of the children. Astride the bull I observe the clouds above. Onward I go, no matter who may wish to call me back.

The bull transcended

Astride the bull, I reach home. I am serene. The bull too can rest. The dawn has come. In blissful repose, within my thatched dwelling I have abandoned the whip and rope (meditation has become part of his being, he need not do anything about enlightenment, he need not do any technique, meditation is his natural state.)

All is one law, not two. We only make the bull a temporary subject. It is as the relation of rabbit and trap, of fish and net. It is as gold and dross, or the moon emerging from a cloud. One path of clear light travels on throughout endless time.

Both bull and self transcended

Whip, rope, person and bull – all merge in No-thing. This heaven is so vast no message can stain it. How may a snowflake exist in a raging fire? Here are the footprints of the patriarchs.

Mediocrity is gone. Mind is clear of limitation. I seek no state of Enlightenment. Neither do I remain where no Enlightenment exists. Since I linger in neither condition, eyes cannot see me. If hundreds of birds strew my path with flowers, such praise would be meaningless.

Reaching the source

Too many steps have been taken returning to the root and the source. Better to have been blind and deaf from the beginning! Dwelling in one's true abode, unconcerned with that without. The river flows tranquilly on and the flowers are red.

From the beginning, truth is clear. Poised in silence, I observe the forms of integration and disintegration. One who is not attached to form need not be reformed. The water is emerald, the mountain is indigo, and I see that which is creating and which is destroying.

In the world

Barefooted and naked of breast, I mingle with people of the world. My clothes are ragged and dust-laden and I am ever blissful. I use no magic to extend my life; now, before me, the trees become alive.

Inside my gate, a thousand sages do not know me. The beauty of my garden is invisible. Why should one search for the footprints of the patriarchs? I go to the marketplace with my bottle (getting drunk with the divine, dance celebrate, being blissful is not enough, one goes back to the world and it becomes a new adventure) and return home with my staff. I visit the wineshop and the market; and everyone I look upon becomes Enlightened.

ACKNOWLEDGMENTS

MARTIN ADAM: 49, 140/141, 158/159

ANCIENT ART & ARCHITECTURE COLLECTION: 34

THE BRIDGEMAN ART LIBRARY: 108/109

BRITISH MUSEUM: 6, 61, 182

DOVER: *Devils, Demons and Witchcraft*: 74 (right), 75 (left)
Japanese Design Motifs: 20, 21, 33, 36, 90, 126
Tibetan and Himalayan Woodblock Prints: 9
Pictorial Archive of Decorative Renaissance Woodcuts: 108

DICK KLEES: 74 (left), 75 (right)

BRUNO KORTENHORST: 11, 12, 17, 22, 28, 30, 36/37, 39, 40, 41, 46, 53, 55, 58, 62, 64/65, 69, 78, 79, 80, 87, 113, 114, 124, 125, 126/7, 128, 131, 134, 135, 139, 147, 148, 154, 160, 162, 163, 164, 165, 168, 169, 172, 174/175, 177, 178, 188, 194/195

CAMERA PRESS: 183, 184

K & B NEWS PHOTO: 143
Brunnello Cappelli: 52, 72
Pier Paolo Chiartosini: 106/107, 130/131, 142, 161
Antonio Sambataro: 120/121
Sergio Gatteschi: 42/43
Antonio Mannu: 170

OSHO MIASTO: 102/103

OSHO INTERNATIONAL FOUNDATION: 2, 16, 48, 60, 82 (all four), 83, 84, 105, (bottom), 151, 152/153, 176, 179, 192, 193

GIANLUCA De SANTIS: 18, 27, 97, 156

ALESSANDRO SARAGOSA: 24, 45

CARMEN STRIDER: 105 (top), 110/111, 122/123

SUSAN B. MORGAN: 56/57

SUSAN GRIGGS AGENCY:
Adam Woolfitt: 14/15
Jim Anderson: 51

JIM WINKLEY: 54, 70/71

Every effort has been made to trace all present copyright holders of the material used in this book, whether companies or individuals. Any omission is unintentional and we will be pleased to correct any errors in future editions of this book.